GOALS TO GOLD

TRADING THE FOOTBALL PITCH FOR THE FINANCIAL MARKETS

BY **LEE SANDFORD**

HARRIMAN HOUSE LTD
3A Penns Road
Petersfield
Hampshire
GU32 2EW
GREAT BRITAIN

Tel: +44 (0)1730 233870
Email: enquiries@harriman-house.com
Website: www.harriman-house.com

First published in Great Britain in 2014
Copyright © Harriman House 2014

The right of Lee Sandford to be identified as Author has been asserted in accordance with the
Copyright, Design and Patents Act 1988.

ISBN: 9780857193568

British Library Cataloguing in Publication Data
A CIP catalogue record for this book can be obtained from the British Library.

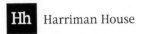 Harriman House

To my mum, dad and brother, for their love and support
and my three daughters
Chloe, Isabelle and Olivia
who bring me so much happiness every day

FREE EBOOK VERSION

As a buyer of the print book of *Goals to Gold* you can now download the eBook version free of charge to read on an eBook reader, your smartphone or your computer. Simply go to:

http://ebooks.harriman-house.com/goalstogold

or point your smartphone at the QRC below.

You can then register and download your free eBook.

CONTENTS

ABOUT THE AUTHOR

DURING A 17-YEAR career in professional football, Lee Sandford played for Portsmouth, Stoke City, Reading, Sheffield United and England's youth team. He played at Wembley, with his whole family watching, and describes this as one of the proudest moments of his life.

Lee enjoyed taking on the responsibility of being a Trade Union representative. He is still involved with football today, playing in the odd charity match and supporting the new charity XPro – which helps ex-footballers of all divisions in life after football.

Following his football career, Lee committed himself to mastering the markets. Like many beginners, the early years saw him attending a few courses, but this generated little more than frustration. So he read avidly and looked further afield. After an enlightening visit to the grains trading pits at the Chicago Board of Trade, he returned to the UK with new vigour.

Lee has now traded for approximately 20 years and for 11 years has earned his living as a trader. In 2009 Lee decided to bring a new style of trading education to the market and started Trading College Ltd. He has personally taught thousands of people to trade the markets for themselves and is delighted by so many success stories from past and present customers.

His 'Trading with Colours' programme has earned him acclaim, resulting in guest appearances at Bloomberg, The London Business School and conferences across Europe. Lee believes in keeping it simple. His best trading strategies are easy to follow but can provide some fantastic trading profits.

Lee has run the London Marathon (in 2009 for Cancer Research) and is the proud father of three daughters.

INTRODUCTION

It takes a great deal of boldness and a great deal of caution to make a great fortune, and when you have got it, it requires ten times as much wit to keep it.

Ralph Waldo Emerson

If I can do it...

IF YOU'D ASKED me 20 years ago what I thought I'd be doing with my life in two-decades' time, the very last thing I would have said is, "writing a book." Not because I didn't want to, but because it would never have occurred to me that I could. I was singularly focused on my career in football for most of my life and latterly became a full-time trader. Writing a book was never on my radar until I realised I had something to say and a good story to tell.

I always knew I wanted to play football and from an early age I believed I had talent. I had never taken my academic education that seriously and my school days had been about sport, sport and more sport. I never looked beyond football. Many people with a clear vision of their future start out with this kind of determined single focus. But life is a long and winding road and when it was time to hang up my boots I had to embrace a new pursuit to keep a roof over my head and provide for my family.

Trading in stocks and shares was something I had done on and off for years. Over the years I had some fantastic windfalls and I had some spectacular losses. Through trial and error I learnt some valuable tricks of the trade. Thus, when I began to think about what I'd like to do with my life when I retired from professional sport, I came to the conclusion that trading was the discipline that, after football, I was most experienced in and passionate about.

I threw myself into learning more and more about finance and trading the markets, and within a few years I had not only become a successful trader, but I also began teaching others how to trade the markets too. When I began to think about finding a platform from which to spread the word about my life and work further afield, writing a book seemed to be the perfect answer, which is how I came to write *Goals to Gold*.

It's not just the content of the book I want to share with you, but the act of writing a book too. This is because it directly relates to my overall message, which is:

If I can do it, anyone can.

Seriously... if a boy from an ordinary South London family, who left school at 16 to become a footballer, can make a great living from trading the markets and go on to write a book about it, then anyone can.

My biggest goal, these days, is to inspire others, which is what I hope to achieve by writing this book.

Humble beginnings

I grew up in a stable, loving family, something I assumed was fairly normal until I got out into the world and started meeting people who came from broken homes. I soon began to realise how fortunate I was. We may not have had a lot of money, but I always had love and stability as well as a great deal of support and encouragement. My parents never pushed me academically, but when I decided it was my dream to become a professional footballer they were behind me every step of the way. This helped instil the right attitude in me from an early age. I worked hard, I was disciplined, and I always appreciated what I had.

This stood me in great stead later in life. When I embarked upon my second career, as a professional trader, I found I was able to draw on the confidence and discipline I'd developed in my early life and in my time as a footballer.

I believe it was the foundations my parents laid for me that gave me the best chance of success in both my careers. When I see people struggling, when I see some of the baggage they carry that holds them back, I wish I could give them the support I had. I see the way their deep-rooted insecurities and lack of true self-confidence create obstacles and I wish I could take those barriers away. Now I have a family of my own, I strive to give them the same comfort and stability that my brother and I got from my mum and dad. I believe that the most important gifts you can give your children are security and the space to learn and develop their unique skills; this will ensure they get the very best start in life.

Learning to ask

At the time of writing, I have a four year-old daughter. I love watching her learn new things, but I have to be patient. When she gets frustrated, I have to stop myself from jumping in and doing the task for her, because I know she will learn faster if she discovers things by herself.

As we get older, we find it harder and harder to learn. That's because most people take comfort from holding on to their preconceived ideas. They don't give themselves the time and space to learn. They don't like to be out of their comfort zone. They don't like to ask why. Why is that so? Do our egos get in the way of our progress? Maybe kids are better at learning because they don't have big egos – they are never afraid to ask questions.

I love learning; I never stop! I'm like a sponge. I love to lap up new ideas, as well as new approaches to old problems. I encourage others to live like this, to keep asking *why* and *how*. It's a rule I live by. If I don't understand something, no matter how embarrassed I might be, I get over my ego and I *ask*. I'm not afraid to keep asking until I understand.

The greatest obstacle that threatens to hold us back in life is our reluctance to learn as we get older. Whether it's learning about new technology, or relearning a damaged thought process, we must continue to learn if we want to progress in life.

Over the years, I've discovered that most people love talking about their fields of expertise. If I want to learn about something new, I find someone who has an extensive knowledge on the subject, then I ask them to help me. I don't think I've ever had anyone say, "No." It's amazing how much you can learn by asking. People *want* to share their knowledge. If you find someone who won't share, chances are they don't really have knowledge to share in that area!

Here's a great example of what I'm talking about.

My nephew plays rugby for London Irish. He recently wrote to the pro who plays in the same position as him for England. My nephew asked this player if he would sit down with him and answer some questions. Guess what... the pro said "Yes!" My nephew subsequently spent an invaluable hour with this guy getting top tips and advice from someone he looked up to, who is one of the greatest experts in his field. If my nephew hadn't asked, this unique opportunity would never have happened.

If you want to learn, teach

I consider myself to be a fairly successful person. I didn't achieve all the goals I reached for, but I made it to some of them. I played for my country, I played at Wembley, I made myself financially independent, and I started a family. I'm happy with my lot. Now I enjoy sharing what I have learned with others who perhaps didn't have the good fortune I had.

I teach people to trade the markets and share my experiences because I want to help reduce the time and energy it will take people to get to where I am. While I believe everyone has their own individual journey to go on – their unique personal learning curve – it doesn't hurt to know how to avoid some of the basic pitfalls. I love sharing the knowledge I've acquired, both from my experiences as a professional footballer and my years of trading. If I can help people jump a couple of rungs up the ladder on their way to being a successful trader, why wouldn't I? I believe anyone can be a success and I'll do whatever I can to help them.

It was actually an accident that I became a teacher. People kept asking me to show them what I did as a trader and I was more than happy to do so. I quickly discovered that I thoroughly enjoyed the process of teaching and this led me to set up a company through which I could teach people. What I didn't bargain for was how I much I would learn myself through the process of teaching.

Teaching others has taught *me* so much about what makes people tick. When I was a footballer I didn't have too much exposure to the general public. Of course I met fans, signed autographs and talked football with them, but I didn't get to meet and talk in depth to a wide range of people from a variety of backgrounds.

Through teaching people to trade the money markets, I've had my eyes opened; it has been a revelation to see that everyone, no matter where they've come from or what they've done, carries their own personal baggage. Many people I would have assumed – judging from their outward appearance and demeanour – were perfectly happy, I discovered were actually feeling miserable and stuck in the rat race, desperate for a way out.

Hearing other people's stories made me realise how relatively lucky I was. I may not have had the formal education or the big accolades, but my solid and happy childhood counted for much more than I gave it credit for.

The big gamble

Trading is not gambling, but trading the markets is a gamble. There are no guarantees, which is why I always urge people not to risk money they cannot afford to lose. If you don't currently have money you can afford to lose, wait until you do.

This is because if you are dependent on trading, it is unlikely to work. You will not be able to make objective decisions in keeping with the rules and structure you have set out. You will put too much pressure on yourself and over trade – that is put trades on when there are no signals telling you to do so.

I passionately believe that *anyone* can learn to trade the markets. (If a guy who doesn't even have a GCSE in maths can do it, anyone can!) You certainly don't need to be a big wig in the city with an Oxford degree in economics to become a successful trader. However, there are some basic traits you need in order to make money as a trader:

1. The **discipline** to follow a set of rules.
2. The **patience** to wait for results.
3. Some disposable **cash** to invest initially.

Be honest with yourself. If you don't think you currently possess all three, please don't try trading the markets until you do. If you do have these three things, in my opinion, you have as good a chance as anybody at making a good return. To be even more blunt, while I believe anyone *can* make money trading the markets, I believe most people – hampered by frustration or fear – will fail.

Trading the markets – and specifically what we will be talking about in this book, spread betting – is not a way to **get rich quick**. Nor is it an immediate **substitute for a salaried job**. But, followed correctly, I believe the strategies I have developed for trading the markets *can* make you an extra monthly income. If you stick with it and learn as you go, and are gradually able to safely risk more sizeable amounts, then that monthly income *could* become quite substantial.

I've watched so many people fail because they won't learn, because they don't take advice, because they walk straight into the pitfalls that have been clearly pointed out to them. They end up losing money they didn't need to lose because they let fear or frustration override their rational thinking.

If you have the **patience** to learn from someone experienced, if you have the **discipline** to stick to a plan – to the rules that you, yourself, have set out – then you can make a nice monthly income from the **cash** you invest.

In summary:

The **bad news** is that there are no guarantees. Even if you follow all the rules there is always an element of risk when you trade the markets.

The **good news** is that you do not need any qualifications or special talents to do it. Everyone has the same, fair chance of being successful at trading.

It's not like there's only one top prize. This isn't *X Factor* or a lottery, with one big prize for the lucky winner; the opportunities and possibilities are more or less unlimited in trading. Trading is more like one long, endless buffet; there is always more space at the table and there is plenty to go around. You can be making the exact same amount as the next person.

Nor is trading a direct competition, such as 100 equally qualified people applying for one job opening. Trading is a job you create yourself. You can start at any time and no one can stop you. There is a wide-open door and there are limitless opportunities.

You don't need innate talent and you don't need to impress any judges! The same information is available to everyone and we all have the same 24 hours in each day. You just have to learn how to use the available information and your available time to your best advantage. That's where I want to help. I want to save you some of that time by sharing my experiences with you and helping you avoid some of the worst pitfalls.

It's all about **money management**. These days, you don't need to know any complicated formulas to manage your money well – modern trading software makes it easier than ever. You still have to make the move, you still have to put the trade on – physically – but you can get software that will tell you exactly what to do and when to do it. You just need the **discipline** to stick to the plan!

Plan to change

If you are happy and totally satisfied with where you are in life, if things are just the way you want them and ticking along nicely, if you have all the money you need and are confident you have everything in place for a secure future, that's fantastic. If not, join the club that most people are in!

If you are not 100% happy, only you can change it. You can't expect other people to do the work for you, or for certain factors to change, magically, overnight. The only way to change or achieve anything in life is to make a plan. Then you need to go about putting that plan into action with drive and a positive attitude. Maybe your plan doesn't work at first. Well, then you adjust it. If you adjust it several times and it still doesn't work, perhaps you need a new plan. You don't abandon the process at the first hurdle.

If you bought a car and it got a flat tyre, you wouldn't dump the car, you'd change the tyre. If it started leaking oil, you'd fix that too. If you found you'd been pouring money into your car for some time and it still wasn't working properly, you might have to abandon it and get a new car, but you would explore all the possibilities to get it running well first. Your plan should be like your car.

People don't usually arrive at their goals following one straight line. We are not computer programs, we are human beings; we get to our destinations through a complex, ever-changing web of processes. Failing is one of those important stages. Maybe you have people in your life who will judge you if you fail, but if you look a little harder you will find many people out there who will respect you for all the efforts you make, for trying again when you don't succeed the first time.

About the book

The book is divided into four parts.

Part One follows the early years of my life and covers my football career. It describes how, having been born into an ordinary family in the south of England, I was spotted at a young age by a local football scout; how I went on to play for my country at youth level and then, in my senior career, played for some of England's oldest clubs, including spending a number of years in the Premier League. This part of the book concludes by describing how my career came to an end a few years after I suffered a serious injury, which prompted me to turn to trading and develop it into my new full-time career.

Part Two delivers a basic introduction to trading the markets and specifically goes into detail about spread betting, the trading vehicle I use. I give some details on how I operate as a trader, the main strategy I use and what I feel are the essential tools of the trade – both in terms of physical tools and psychological approach.

Part Three covers in detail some of the most poignant experiences I've had as a trader. These are some of my best *trading stories*. These stories provide even more insight into my decision-making process, and show how I deal with some of the daily ups and downs of being a professional trader.

Part Four shows some of the parallels between trading and football. By drawing on my knowledge and experience from the world of football, I describe how and why certain pitfalls present themselves in trading and the best way to deal with them.

It was always my aim to provide something that had entertainment as well as educational value while I was writing this book. So, read and learn, but I hope you enjoy parts of the story too!

PART ONE

THE FOOTBALL YEARS

CHAPTER ONE:
HAMPSHIRE HEAVEN

Early days in Elephant and Castle

MY FIRST MEMORY of playing football is a somewhat painful one. I was five and my brother Paul was nine. Paul and his friends met up every Saturday to play football on a big concrete area near where we lived. It was probably a series of disused tennis courts that had doubled as netball courts – the kind of nasty, hard surface that could really mess up a kid's face. I would go along with my dad, who acted as their referee and coach, and watch from the sidelines.

One Saturday I begged dad to let me play and he said I could. I was so excited; I knew I had a lot to prove to these big lads and if I played well, they'd let me play again. Everything was riding on my first appearance. I had been playing one-touch football with Paul and our cousin Chris in our six-foot long front yard and I was confident I could control the ball.

I got put on just before half time and hovered around in centre midfield, waiting for my big moment. Finally it came. Craig Andrews passed me the ball. I caught it easily with my left foot, turned and started dribbling down the left wing. Two seconds later I felt intense pain and heard a big crack. The next thing I knew, I was lying on the ground with dad looking down at me.

I'd knocked myself out. I'd been so busy watching the ball and trying to keep control of it, I hadn't seen some small goal posts down the wings (presumably erected for a 5-a-side game that would be played on the width of the main pitch). I'd run straight into one of these hard, metal posts and given myself an almighty crack on the head. That was my excuse for not doing well at academic subjects at school sorted; I lost half my brain cells when I was five!

At the time, we were living over a pub in Elephant and Castle where dad was working as a publican. For a place named after a pub, Elephant and Castle lived up to its name as a boozy, petty crime-ridden London borough on the south side of the river, just east of Waterloo. In the early 1970s, the area was still recovering from the extensive bombing it suffered during the Second World War, which had left many people having to double and triple up with their extended families in large Victorian town houses and prefabs.

The general overcrowding and lack of space in London had led the government to spearhead several relocation projects. Keen to get us out of the rundown place we were living in, and give us a bigger and better home, my parents applied for one in Basingstoke.

Move to Basingstoke

Basingstoke is an old Hampshire market town about 50 miles southwest of London. Hampshire County Council had done a deal with London to take some of their overspill and had undertaken a huge new building project. There were housing developments springing up all over the countryside that surrounded Basingstoke. The deal was if you could get a local job, the council would automatically rehouse you.

Looking back to the time just before we moved, Paul was beginning to get into a bit of trouble with our older cousins and local lads. As I looked up to my older brother so much, I have no doubt I would have soon followed in his footsteps. To give Paul and me a better start in life by moving us out of London, my parents had to sacrifice their own social lives, and the proximity to their support network of family and friends. It must have been tough for them, especially at the start, but they may have saved their sons from a life of petty crime and pretty poor prospects.

When dad managed to get a job as a security guard in a large company based in Basingstoke, we were guaranteed a new home in the local area, but the houses and school weren't quite ready. Dad had to start his new job and give up the pub meaning we temporarily had nowhere to live, so we moved in with my nan for a few months. I was sharing a bed with my brother, we only had an outside toilet and our bath was in the kitchen. It was a far cry from the glamorous life of a professional footballer that I was already starting to dream of!

The first thing that hit me when we finally moved out to Basingstoke was how much space there was. There was the modest development of houses, a school, some shops, and then miles and miles of space for as far as the eye could see. For a kid who wants to run and run, it was heaven. Unlike my parents (I'm sure), I don't remember missing London for a moment. I was too young for that kind of nostalgic longing. All I could see was the benefit of moving out of the big, overcrowded city and having endless clean, green space to run around in. Once I saw that, I never looked back.

The other thing that was all clean, shiny and new was our school. It had only been open for about three or four years, so Paul's class, Year Four, comprised the oldest kids in the school. There was no old gang ruling the roost, there was no graffiti or broken equipment. It was ours for the taking.

Furthermore, our sports fields seemed endless. No more playing football on concrete courts; there was lush, green grass everywhere. I quickly became a sports nut. I was good at everything: cricket, football, running, rugby; basically, if it involved running, I was good at it. I was the school sports captain in the making. I was never happier than when I was outside, running around and getting muddy. Of course, this helped detract from the fact I was absolutely useless at my schoolwork!

Weekends in London had been spent hanging around the pub being told not to get in the way; Saturdays and Sundays were dad's busiest times, with only a few hours off to spend with his kids. By contrast, weekends in our new home were about walking for miles and miles across green fields, and hanging out with dad for hours on end, bird watching through his top-notch binoculars. We were immersed in nature; it was fast becoming an idyllic childhood as far as I was concerned.

Getting serious about football

I probably got more serious about football over other sports because of my best friend at the time, Matt. We'd met at primary school and that's where we first got really keen on football. Matt's dad ran the local football team, so as soon as we were old enough and good enough, Matt and I were recruited. By the time we were approaching our teens, we had become local football heroes, playing games every weekend. We were always entering and winning tournaments, leading to cabinets full of trophies and medals.

My dad was instrumental in making it possible for me to play so much football at an early age. He would drive me to practice every Tuesday, and to all the weekend games; he was on my side every step of the way. The only thing dad and I seriously fell out over was our football teams. He supported Chelsea. In defiance, and partly because we had an uncle, Jim, who worked at White Hart Lane, Paul and I had chosen Spurs. My Uncle Jim was a great guy. He sadly passed away recently, but he left a real legacy behind him; many of my family members (myself, Paul, and many of our cousins) are all still huge Spurs fans.

Mum's support was crucial too. Without her, I wouldn't have had any kit to play in! Us boys would pile out of the house on a Sunday morning and return several hours later, happy, exhausted and covered in mud. There would be baths run, the washing machine would be loaded up with our filthy clothes, and there would be a big Sunday roast on the table by three o'clock.

My parents never put much pressure on me in terms of my schoolwork. They simply said, "Do your best, son. As long as you do your best, that's fine with us." Looking back, I think what I actually heard was, "Do as little as you can get away with." I know my friends got punishments and lost privileges for not doing their homework, but mum and dad were pretty laid back with me. I seem to remember getting a CSE in Pottery and Art, but that was about it from my time at school. I often ask myself if I regret the fact that my parents didn't push me harder to get a better education. Maybe it would have given me other opportunities, but perhaps I would have rebelled anyway. My head was filled with sport; there was no room for anything else.

There was another big reason why I lacked the motivation and incentive to try hard academically... I knew I had a job lined up as soon as I hit 16. That must have played a major part in how little I did in school.

TEAM PHOTO FROM MY CHILDHOOD CLUB BEECHDOWN FC

Interest from Southampton and Portsmouth

At the age of 13, I was already on the books at Southampton, which meant they were seriously considering giving me a schoolboy contract once I turned 14. This would have tied me to them for two years, but wouldn't necessarily guarantee me a paid apprentice contract at 16, which is what any young, hopeful footballer is looking for.

A few months after I turned 13, I went away for a week for the Hampshire trials. It was hugely exciting as it was my first real trip away from my home and family, and it meant playing football non-stop for a whole week. At that point, football-obsessed as I was, it was my dream come true. I clearly remember watching the royal wedding of Prince Charles and Lady Di while I was at the trials, so this must have been late July 1981. I arrived home from the trials tired but exhilarated, with the whole summer stretching ahead of me. All I could think about was football, about how many hours of playing I could fit in over the summer holidays.

The following week we were sitting down to dinner on an ordinary Thursday night and there was a knock on the door. It was Dave Hirst, a scout for Portsmouth Football Club (PFC), Southampton's biggest rivals. He told me he'd been watching me at the Hampshire trials and that Portsmouth wanted me to sign schoolboy forms with them. I wasn't sure. While I wasn't that happy at Southampton, I felt like it would be disloyal to sign with Portsmouth. I knew Southampton was expecting me to sign schoolboy forms with them once I turned 14.

Seeing my hesitation, Dave pulled out his trump card. He told me if I signed the schoolboy forms with Portsmouth, they would guarantee me an apprentice contract when I turned 16. I was still only 13, so I couldn't sign the schoolboy forms until I turned 14, but Dave said I could go down to Portsmouth that summer and see what I thought. If I liked it, I could sign with them when I turned 14 the following April, with a guaranteed contract at 16.

Southampton hadn't made that guarantee so it was a massive pull. Plus, as I'd told dad only a few months before, I wasn't really enjoying myself at Southampton anymore. I wasn't feeling challenged there; it was becoming too monotonous. I wasn't even sure anymore that I wanted to stick it out for two more years as a schoolboy at Southampton. Dad encouraged me to do whatever I thought would make me happy. So in the end it wasn't a hard choice. Once I turned 14, I signed the forms with Portsmouth.

Clearly, I owe a lot to Dave Hirst. He saw potential in me and supported me throughout my time at Portsmouth. He had a keen eye for talent and helped to identify and develop many young players, such as Spurs midfielder and England player Darren Anderton.

I had to keep it a big secret at school; I couldn't tell anyone about the contract I'd signed with Portsmouth that was going to allow me to leave, with a guaranteed job, at 16. Now, of course, I had an excuse to slack off my schoolwork completely. Why did I need an education when I knew I had a job to go to? I wasn't cocky, but I didn't worry if I got in trouble for not working hard enough. I knew something they didn't know... that I didn't need an education. Or so I thought in my naïve, football-obsessed teenage mind.

The future contract did keep me out of trouble in other ways. For teenagers who aren't particularly academic, there are always too many distractions and temptations. It's the same in any generation. In my day, glue sniffing was the drug of choice, but in every generation there will be those unhealthy choices that kids can make that will jeopardise their chances of getting a good education.

Sport plays such an important role in keeping kids focused on something healthy and away from smoking and drugs; they need a physical outlet. I remember plenty of parties during my teenager years – there were girls, there was beer – but nothing was more important to me than football. The best thing we can do for our kids is to keep them involved in sport, to keep physical exercise a big part of their lives, giving them something to focus on outside of schoolwork. But maybe not at the expense of it, as it became for me!

In my last two years at school, I was in serious training. Dad used to drive me to all my practices and games. He had been working as a postman for a few years by then. He would do a night shift from 11pm until 4am, sleep a few hours during the day, and then drive me to practice before going to work again. There's no way I would have been able to do any of it without the help and support of my parents. I am forever grateful to them for all they did.

Paul got the same support, and he played for Basingstoke for a while, but his heart wasn't invested quite as deeply as mine. I'm sure he could have made it as a professional player too if he'd pushed himself, but he had other, stronger interests. He was always very supportive of me, though, coming to games and proudly cheering me on.

Of course we had our brotherly fights, meaning proper physical fights. He was the older brother, I was the annoying little brother, so he was always telling me to get lost and stop bothering him, which obviously goaded me on. Dad would drag us off each other telling us we had to stop fighting and be kinder to each other because we were brothers; his own brother had fled to Australia in slightly dubious circumstances and he'd hardly seen him as an adult, so he wanted Paul and me to be close and appreciate each other. We did appreciate each other deep down. But we were also average teenage boys who showed their love through giving each other bruises and black eyes.

Hampshire Cross Country Championships

I had an early lesson in dealing with criticism and overcoming challenges. At the age of 14, I returned home from a training camp down in Portsmouth and Dave Hirst was soon on the phone to my dad telling him I had to work on my fitness. Other players were fitter and I had to do something about it.

You would expect most sporty youngsters to be athletic and fit but you need to raise the bar if you want to make it at the top. I was surprised when Dave called but I wanted to be the best player I could possibly be and I was determined that I would do anything to increase my fitness levels.

So what do you do if you're a dad and you have just been told your son is not fit enough? You enter him in the Hampshire Cross Country Championships for under 14s! This was a three-race competition, over a month. The Championship medal winner was determined by the average position over the three races. I was up against all the best runners in the county under the age of 14 who had, in all probability, run these distances many times before. The only time I had done anything like this was in school PE when we went around Down Grange fields. It was always muddy and wet.

The first race was no different. The rain had been falling and the course was full of mud. The first race was a shock to the system but I went on to come first against a field of nearly 60 teenagers. In the second race I knew what to expect and, even though I felt nervous, I went on to win that race too. So now I had won the first two races and only had to come in the first three on the final race to be crowned champion. And this is what I did.

The third race didn't go as planned but I still finished in the first three and was duly announced as the Hampshire Cross Country Champion for the under 14s. I remember finishing the last race and sitting down on the soggy grass to take my spikes off, saying to dad "I'm never doing that again!" My dad laughed. We often speak about that day still.

Apprenticeship begins

As soon as I turned 16, I signed my apprentice contract with Portsmouth and left school without looking back. It was one of the proudest moments of my life, turning up at Portsmouth Football Club's ground, Fratton Park, for my very first day as a professional footballer along with all the other lads who were starting that season. We already knew each other because we'd all been playing on schoolboy contracts for the youth team for a couple of years, so there was a great atmosphere; it was incredibly exciting.

Mum and dad drove me to the ground and I was taken to the boardroom along with the other new apprentices to sign all the paperwork and complete the formalities, which included having our photos taken. We were all wearing our best suits and feeling very grown up.

We all got a signing fee of £200. I gave my fee to mum and dad; I knew they wanted a new stereo and it would help to pay for that. I wanted to show them how grateful I was; they'd helped make my dream of becoming a professional footballer come true. I could never thank them enough for that. As they drove away, I had a real lump in my throat and a tear in my eye. Up to this point in my life, they'd always been there; now, for the first time in my life, I was alone. I was a professional, a grown up, I had to knuckle down and do my apprenticeship. I was excited, but more than a little nervous.

I shared my first digs with my mate, Brendan O'Connell, an Irish lad who'd grown up in London. He was cool. We had so many laughs together and with the family we lived with. We got a weekly wage of £26 and I felt rich. All our living expenses – basically food and board – were paid for by the club, so the £26 was just spending money. It went pretty far in those days.

The main objective was to work towards getting a professional contract; that was the goal of every apprentice. At the start, I was just happy to be there. I couldn't believe I was getting paid, every week, for doing something I loved. I knew I was fortunate in that. I never took it for granted.

So that was it. At the age of 16, I left school and started the next adventure of my life, as an apprentice at Portsmouth Football Club. That's where I met one of the greatest mentors of my life: Alan Ball.

CHAPTER TWO:
ON THE BALL

Getting to know Alan

As THE YOUNGEST member of England's 1966 World Cup winning team, no one knew about the pressures on young footballers better than Alan Ball. He was in charge of Portsmouth's youth team when I joined and he immediately became my mentor.

I'd known Alan for a while already by then. He would often come and watch the Portsmouth schoolboy training sessions and chat to my dad while I was training. He and dad got along great, which helped to reassure me as I adjusted to living away from home for the first time. My dad's opinion was important to me, so it was natural for me to respect someone dad liked and respected too. I looked up to Alan and came to regard him as my *football dad*.

You never knew who you might meet when you were with Alan. Before I'd started my apprenticeship, when I was 15 and still at school, I'd been asked to play for the Portsmouth reserves a couple of times. If the squad was down a few players, due to injuries, one of the reserve team would go up to play for the first team, and then I got to play for the reserves. Even though I was 15 and still on a schoolboy contract, Alan believed I could hold my own against seasoned professionals. It was great experience.

On one occasion when they needed me to play, for some reason dad wasn't able to get me there, so Alan offered to pick me up and bring me back after the game. He arrived at our house in his big fancy Mercedes. I remember sitting in the back and dreaming of owning one some day. I thought maybe if I stuck around Alan, some of his success might rub off on me.

The game went well that night. We must have won because I remember being in a great mood before we left. As we were getting in the car, Alan told me we had to drive over to the other side of the pitch before we set off home, because someone was waiting to talk to him. I could see this man in the distance but, at that point, I didn't think much of it. Nothing could have prepared me for what happened next!

We drove around the ground and pulled up where this man was standing. He got into the passenger seat next to Alan and turned around to say hello to me. I couldn't believe my eyes – it was Bobby Moore! The captain of England's 1966 World Cup winning team was sitting right in front of me; he was saying hello to me. Then Alan introduced us so now he knew my name. Bobby Moore knew my name! I was stunned.

I sat back in my seat as Alan and Bobby talked, thinking it must mean something that I was there. The three of us, Alan Ball, Bobby Moore and I, were sitting together in a Mercedes. In that moment, there was no doubt in my mind that I must be destined for some kind of greatness. Surely I would be playing for England one day. It had to be a sign!

* * *

On the apprenticeship at Portsmouth we had quite a gruelling daily schedule, but as far as I was concerned, I was living the life of Riley.

We started our day at 9am every morning doing our apprenticeship jobs. When the first team turned up an hour later, we would all start training. In those days, apprentices really earned their keep. We scrubbed the toilets, we painted the terraces, we cleaned the boots of the first team members, and we took pride in our work. No one ever complained; it was an honour to be there. I can't imagine asking a 16 year-old member of a Premiership youth team to go and scrub the toilets these days.

It was exciting to be away from home, I'd been itching to leave and get out into the world, to explore a bit, and be myself. I suddenly felt like an adult; at home I'd always been a kid. Even so, I was very homesick and called home whenever I could. I would often sneak up to the press box when no one was around and use the phones in there. I'd call mum and dad, and my friends. I would never admit how much I missed my parents, but I'm sure mum could hear it in my voice. No one could actually admit to being homesick, but I have no doubt all the other young lads were feeling it too.

Luckily I was never away from home for too long because I went back every weekend. On Saturday dad would drive down and watch me in the morning's youth team game and then we'd drive home. If the first team were playing a home game, we'd stay and watch that and drive home after.

I was always itching to go out with my mates as soon as I got home. My parents would be dying to hear all my news about how I was getting on and how training was going, but all I wanted to do was get out of the house as fast as possible and meet everyone in town. Looking back, I feel quite bad that I didn't spend more time with them, especially now I have kids of my own and know how it feels to wish you could share every single moment of their lives. I'm sure all teenagers are the same though; I'd get in, bolt down my dinner, answer questions as quickly and briefly as possible, and then get ready to go out.

Getting ready was a process in itself. It was the big summer of 1984 and everyone had to look the part. Every girl had to dress like Madonna and every boy like George Michael. Madonna was *Like a Virgin*, Laura Branigan had no *Self Control*; we heard *99 Red Balloons*, *Time After Time*, and Billy Ocean and Lionel Richie battled it out in the Top 10. If the Duran Duran *Wild Boys* got out of hand, who were you gonna call? *Ghostbusters*. I had my Simon Le Bon highlights and my *Footloose* moves. I had money in my pocket and was on my way to becoming a huge football star – as far as I was concerned, I was going to play for England one day. Life was great.

The gaffer (as football managers are called by players) instilled in us his philosophy of "you work hard so you can play hard." While there was definitely a bit of a laddish culture – of going out, drinking and chatting up women – it was never done at the expense of training and playing our best.

Alan also taught us the great value of preparation. To this day, I can't do anything unless I'm totally prepared. I have to complete my research and be satisfied I've practised hard enough, that everything is ready and in its place, or I can't do my job – whatever it may be.

An essential part of pre-game preparation for a footballer is to have clean boots. You can't start a game with old, hard mud caked on to your studs. As apprentices at PFC, we were all assigned pros and told we were responsible for keeping their boots clean. My pros were Mick Kennedy and Mick Tait. I made sure their boots were spotless every day. I was also in charge of cleaning the changing rooms of the away teams on a Saturday afternoon, which led to my next exciting encounter with a football legend.

It happened after a home game against Nottingham Forest. We'd beaten them and most of them had already sloped off, heads hung low, back to their coach. I went down to clean up their changing room before I headed home. It was cold, so I had my coat on, also ready for a quick getaway. I wasn't cutting any corners though; that dressing room had to be spotless.

As I entered, mop and bucket in hand, I saw there were still two men sitting over in the corner. I soon recognised them as Brian Clough and Des Walker (the future England defender); they were having a post-match chat. Brian Clough was already something of a legend by then; well on his way to becoming known as "the greatest manager England never had." I started mopping the floor.

After a couple of minutes, Brian Clough called over to me in his familiar Middlesbrough accent, "Hey, young man, young man," he said. "You take your coat off while you're doing the cleaning. Your mum and dad won't appreciate it if you get it dirty. They spent a lot of money on that coat." I can remember that moment like it was yesterday. But there was an even bigger moment about to happen.

England youth team

One afternoon, Alan Ball asked all the players to assemble in our home team changing room for a meeting. We didn't know what it was for and we were sure someone had got into trouble. So when he asked me to come out to the front and stand beside him, I was terrified. I saw he had a letter in his hand and I thought maybe some local girl's mum had written to say I'd been out with her daughter and I was never to go near her again.

He gave me the letter and asked me to read it out. As soon as I saw the three lions on the headed paper, my heart lifted. It was from the FA. I started reading and soon I was saying the words, "...pleased to announce that Lee Sandford has been selected to play for the England Youth team." The clapping and cheering from my teammates rang in my ears for days.

The first game I played for the England youth team was against the Republic of Ireland in 1986. It was due to be played at Hillsborough, Sheffield Wednesday's home ground, where we did a few training sessions. At the last moment, due to heavy snow in Sheffield, the game was moved to Leeds, to Elland Road. Mum and dad were obviously incredibly proud and determined to come and watch me. They drove all the way from Basingstoke to Leeds. I think it was the furthest dad had ever driven.

Standing on the pitch before kick-off, singing the national anthem, I thought I was dreaming. This was the moment I'd watched so many times on TV, in every cup final, with all the players lined up singing *God Save The Queen*. Now I was doing it, with my parents watching me from somewhere in the stands. I could have burst with pride.

I was in a team with players who went on to be some of the greatest footballers of my generation. I remember Paul Ince was there, as was Neil "Razor" Ruddock. We won 2-0 and there were huge celebrations on the coach after the match, and back at the hotel, well into the night. Mum and dad were there to enjoy it as well. It was a momentous occasion.

The next game was a month or so later and was against Scotland, played in Aberdeen. Then we started the preparations for our forthcoming tour to China. I was over the moon when I got picked to be in the squad going to China. I remember having to go and get my visa stamped in my passport, and being measured up for my suit. And then something happened.

I don't remember exactly who left, who took over, or what the issues were, but there was a change of management and the new manager wanted to pick a slightly different squad. This time I wasn't selected. I was absolutely devastated, but there was nothing I could do about it.

Looking back now, I can see how it was my first experience of being a pawn in someone else's agenda. Whoever the new manager was, he wanted to make his own selection of players, to put his own stamp on the squad, so I, along with several others, got dropped.

It was a sobering experience, but it taught me how ephemeral professional success can be. It showed me that there are no guarantees in life. It was also my first lesson in letting go of control, in understanding that you cannot always be in charge of what happens to you. Little did I know then that I would use that lesson when it came to accepting the way money markets work; that I would use the story to show people how they have been pawns in the game played by big bankers and global economies.

Only now, with hindsight, can I see how valuable such experiences are to a young person, how early disappointments can actually give you the tools you need in order to succeed in life. Moments like this helped me develop the skills I would one day need to become a disciplined and unemotional trader.

Turning pro

It wasn't altogether a bad time. I had plenty of successes to take my mind off the England youth squad disappointment. It was the season that PFC got into the First Division (what is now called the Premier League), and

I had recently been named as the FA's Young Player of the Month, a very prestigious award for a young player. In my second season at PFC my wages had gone up to £35 a week. I thought I was rich, but I had no idea what was on the cards for me.

Most apprentices saw out their two years before signing professional forms, but before my two years were up, when I was only 17, I was offered a professional contract at £250 a week. In today's terms that sounds like nothing, but imagine a pay rise of over *seven* times your current weekly salary! The money still meant nothing to me, I was just happy to be playing football every day, but I was able to start buying real, grown-up assets like stereos and cars... and eventually my first property.

My first game as a professional was at Millwall, ironically the closest league club to Elephant and Castle. I was on the bench initially, but soon after the start of the game Kenny Swain got injured and I went on. In those days there were high mesh fences all around the pitch because football hooliganism was a big problem. I was terrified as I ran out on to the pitch because I could see the Millwall fans pushing up against the fence.

They were like snarling tigers, eager to get out of their cage and tear apart their prey. I was still a victim of the 1980s and with my long, bleached-blonde Nik Kershaw hairstyle, I was a prime target for the Millwall fans. They started chanting and shouting abuse at me, spitting and calling me a "fucking Portsmouth poofter." I desperately wanted to turn around and tell them that I was born up the road, that I was a local lad, just like them, but I knew it wouldn't have made a difference. More importantly, I had to concentrate on my first professional game.

In the end, we beat the home team 4-0. It was such an impressive victory that some of the Millwall fans actually clapped us off the pitch. Even so, there were some very angry fans lining the street on the way back to the coach and I remember being quite scared, imagining they were going to drag me off and beat me to a pulp. Luckily Noel Blake pulled me out of harm's way. At 6'2", and with shoulders almost as wide, he was a force to be reckoned with and the angry fans backed off. Noel and I became great mates after that; it was the beginning of a lifelong friendship.

Alan Ball continued to be my mentor and my greatest inspiration as I rose through the ranks. He would give the most incredible pre-match motivational speeches. He could actually make you cry. I remember choking back tears several times at the end of some of his pep talks. He made you feel like the only thing that existed was the game you were about to play. To this day, I think he is the best motivator I have ever met. Of course, his influence didn't end on the pitch. His "live hard, play hard" attitude encouraged us to enjoy ourselves to excess after the game. All the drinking and partying was fine as long as we'd worked hard out on the pitch.

Alan had a reputation for gathering up mavericks that other clubs had grown exasperated with and getting them focused. Perhaps it was because he allowed us to get away with so much partying off the pitch that we worked so hard in training and during the matches. We were known as "the gremlins" because we were never out of trouble, whether it was on the pitch or in the pub. After hours, it was a constant flow of booze and girls. There was a fantastic team spirit and I never questioned it for a moment. You couldn't, you were part of a team; the peer pressure was huge.

First Division

Being promoted to the First Division in the 1986-87 season meant we would now be playing the country's top clubs. In the mid-80s, the greatest club in the land was undoubtedly Liverpool.

In 1986, Liverpool was at the top of the top division and had held the title for three consecutive years shortly before that. In the season just before we were promoted they had won "the double" (the league and the FA Cup). They were untouchable. When I realised I was going to be playing at Anfield, I could hardly believe it. For years I'd been watching players like Ian Rush, Alan Hansen, Mark Lawrenson and my all-time favourite, Kenny Dalglish, playing on TV. These guys were my football heroes. Now I was going to be meeting them face-to-face. I had never felt so much pressure.

As I came down the steps in the tunnel and saw the famous This is Anfield sign for the first time, my knees were already shaking. As usual, we had arrived a couple of hours before the game and were headed out on to the pitch to do our pre-match warm up. At an hour and a half before kick off in most football clubs in England, you won't find a soul in the stands. At Anfield, as we emerged from the tunnel to go and warm up, I couldn't believe my eyes. The Kop (the stand where Liverpool's most passionate supporters congregate) was completely full.

Another distinctive thing about Liverpool fans is that they don't boo the opposition, they whistle at them. In some ways it's almost more unnerving. And I'm sure it contributed to creating what turned out to be the worst moment of my career to date.

I was marking the Australian midfielder, Craig Johnston (who went on to design the popular Predator football boot made by Adidas). He wasn't that tall, but his mass of black curly hair made him seem taller and more threatening. He had an imposing presence about him. Looking back now, I can identify it as unshakeable confidence, something I sorely lacked as I waited for kick-off.

By the time the referee blew his whistle and the game got started, I was in a state of shock. I froze. I literally got stage fright. The next 90 minutes were a blur. I completely bottled it. I never went anywhere near the ball. I felt like I had lead boots on; it was a struggle to get one foot in front of the other.

Luckily, because we were getting so badly hammered by the home team, my abysmal performance wasn't so noticeable, but I was shattered by it. I felt terrible. Any confidence I had ever possessed had disappeared and I was left with nothing but my fears. Play for England? Me? "Don't be stupid," my inner voice was saying. "You're not even good enough to play at Anfield. Who do you think you are?"

Mental strength

For years I wondered what on earth happened at Anfield that day. What caused me to lose my nerve so completely? Whenever I had to approach events in life that scared me, I thought of that moment. Now, I realise I became overwhelmed by the pressure. In my mind I had this perception that I didn't deserve to be out there, that I wasn't good enough to be on the same pitch as my heroes, these giants of football.

This was my first lesson in understanding the concept of the mental game. You can be physically fit and prepared, and have all the best intentions in the world, but if on the day, in the moment, you listen to those voices of doubt, you're doomed.

These days, most sports training programmes encompass an element of psychological preparation, but back then, apart from the pre-game pep talk, it was a fairly new concept. There were no sports psychologists helping you overcome mental blocks. There was a focus on the team spirit, of course, but there was no one to tell you what to do with your own individual fears; to teach you how to confront those voices that rise up in you at the worst moments, saying, "You're going to fail, you can't do this," or, "You're going to make a fool of yourself, everybody's going to laugh at you."

It was the only time in my football life that this happened to me, that I froze and was unable, on any level, to pull something out of the bag. It never happened again, but thinking back to that moment still gives me chills today.

The next time I experienced something close to that paralysing sensation of fear, I was older and in a different career. This time, it was a fear of public speaking. It was a strange concept, to be afraid of being in front of people, because I'd played football in front of thousands of people and I'd always enjoyed performing to a crowd. There's nothing like that huge roar from the fans when you're winning. Speaking to people was a whole different ball game for me though.

When it happened, when I froze up in fear just before I was due to give a lecture to a group of traders a few years ago, I immediately sought help. I managed to get some great training to help me battle those fears, those voices of doubt that can destroy even the most talented people.

I stayed at PFC for three more seasons. By the time I was 21, Alan Ball had left and gone to Stoke City. Our new manager was John Gregory. We'd just been relegated so spirits were low. Plus, Gregory brought with him a whole batch of new players. Things were changing and I missed the old days.

A phone call came through the day before the PFC Christmas party in 1989 – it was Alan Ball asking me if I wanted to sign with Stoke. At that point I was out of contract with PFC, so I didn't hesitate for one moment before saying yes. I packed my bags and drove to Stoke the next day.

CHAPTER THREE:
THE EMOTIONAL DECISION

Starting out in the Potteries

AS I DROVE up the M6 to Staffordshire, I kept thinking about how far from home I was going to be. In my mind I had imagined Stoke being, at most, two hours drive from Portsmouth. I was 21. I had never driven myself such a long distance before. By the time I got to Birmingham, which had taken the full two hours, I was certain Stoke had to be just around the corner. When I was still driving 45 minutes later, I started to panic slightly.

Despite the fact that I knew I was going to be miles and miles from everyone and everywhere I knew, I felt sure I was doing the right thing. I was nervous but my loyalty to Alan was so strong I never questioned my decision. I hadn't thought about what was best for my career, about whether it was wise to move down a division (at the time, Stoke were in Division Two, the second tier of the football league system) or whether any other club might be interested in me; I went with my heart. I didn't want anyone else as my manager, I just wanted to play under Alan, my football dad.

It was an emotional decision and any good businessperson will tell you that you shouldn't allow your emotions to dictate your business decisions. At that point I didn't see myself as a business, which might have been my mistake. I absolutely loved every minute of my time at Stoke and I was never happier under any manager than I was under Alan Ball, but it's possible that a different decision at this early stage in my career might have led to bigger and better things for me in the grand scheme. However, at the time, I never gave it a second thought. I was, literally, having a ball.

The Stoke fans were fantastic and couldn't have been more welcoming to me. Also, it wasn't long before the gaffer started to bring up other PFC players, so some of the old crowd were together again and we tried to recreate the atmosphere we'd had in Portsmouth. There was a sense of security in things staying the same.

But times were a-changing and the old "work hard so you can play hard" philosophy wasn't quite producing the results anymore. Either that, or other clubs were doing away with it and getting more serious, leaving us in their wake as they moved up the league tables. Coaching tactics were being overhauled and modernised. While we were having fun, my old football dad was falling a little behind the times. At the end of my first season at Stoke, under Alan Ball's management, we were relegated to the Third Division.

To be honest, at this time, I wasn't too bothered about where we were in the league, I just wanted to play football every day and collect my weekly wages. I had other responsibilities to think about by then... it wasn't just about me anymore.

Seeking stability

Shortly before I signed with Stoke, my beautiful daughter Chloe was born. Her mum and I had only been together for a short time and, sadly, the relationship didn't last. As any parent will tell you, the birth of a child changes your life, irreversibly, forever.

A big part of my focus now had to be on my job security and I knew I had to keep earning my living as a footballer. I had no other qualifications; I wasn't trained to do anything else. Playing for Stoke City was safe – I knew I would always be welcome and wanted at Stoke. Maybe a part of me had been thinking with my head when I signed with

Stoke after all because at this stage in my life, with my responsibilities, it wasn't so much about playing for England and the glory anymore, it was about having a steady job and providing for my dependents. I doubt I could provide particularly well for a family on the jobs I could get with my CSE in Woodwork, or my O-levels in Pottery and Art!

When you're 16, you can't imagine being 21, let alone 31 or 41. When I was at school, I believed all I would ever need to do in life was to keep being good at football. I thought that, as long as I kept fit, stuck to the training regime and did my best out on the pitch, that I would always have a job. However, once I'd been out in the real world for several years, reality hit home. I saw players retire, get injured and get the sack. It occurred to me that you can't depend on talent alone and that there will always be mitigating factors outside of your control. I realised that if anything ever happened to stop me from playing football, I'd have nothing to fall back on. It scared the hell out of me.

So when the PFA (the Professional Footballers Association, the footballers' trade union) announced a scheme to give young footballers the opportunity to get a university degree, I jumped at the chance and in the autumn of 1995 I arrived at Manchester Metropolitan University's Alsager campus with 14 other local footballers and football-related professionals, including coaches. The degree was in Sports Science and Coaching. I didn't have a clue what to expect. On our first day, the lecturer told us all to go off to the library and choose a book. We could choose anything we wanted but, once we had picked something, we had to bring it back to the room and read a passage out loud to our fellow students.

I was browsing the shelves of the library when I felt a tap on the shoulder. It was one of my old mates from my Portsmouth days who'd signed with Stoke around the same time I had. He looked miserable. He told me he couldn't hack it – he didn't have the balls to read something out loud in front of all the other guys. He quit on the spot; he didn't even come back to the lecture room that day.

For me, this opportunity came at exactly the right time in my life. I was ready to learn again. I was 27 and I'd had an amazing six years at Stoke, playing football and having fun, but I knew my big partying days were behind me. I had to plan for the future and this seemed like a great way to begin.

It was tough going, being back at school after more than ten years! Out of the 15 of us who started, only about half of us graduated. I was glad I stayed the course. Apart from anything else, it taught me that there is nothing to be gained from quitting. Quitting is actually the easiest thing in the world to do. It's easy to hit a wall and give up, declaring, "I can't do this." We will even kid ourselves that we don't want to do something just as an excuse not to finish it.

All of us who started that degree were out of our comfort zones. We knew the football pitch, not the library stacks, but those of us who stuck it out were well rewarded. It's one thing in life doing the thing you always believed you were destined to do, but there is nothing like the feeling of being awarded something you were fairly convinced you could never achieve.

There were other new influences in my life around this time. I was in a steady relationship with an older woman who taught me a great deal about life and business. It was probably my first, proper adult relationship and it grounded me. She was a fitness instructor and had opened her own health club right in the middle of the late 1990s fitness boom. She was a successful businesswoman and I learnt business practices and skills from her that I still use today.

Future planning

Graduating from university changed me; it shifted my focus. I suddenly became a sponge. I wanted to learn everything I could about everything there was to know. It had finally dawned on me that being a professional footballer was not a career that could last forever. Okay, the Steven Gerrards of this world probably don't need fall-back plans, but most of the rest of us will have a nasty bump as we come back down to earth if we don't plan for the future.

Sadly, few footballers have this fact pressed upon them with anything like the importance it needs. At the time of writing there have been several articles in the press drawing attention to the fact that many ex-professional footballers are in severe financial difficulty, if not bankrupt. Furthermore, there are no less than 100 former footballers behind bars.

If more emphasis was put on teaching them additional skills that they could use when their football careers come to an end, or on how to invest the large sums of money they earn in their most prolific years in order to ensure a more secure financial future, it would only be a good thing. Guidance regarding alternative careers and financial planning should be as important as the careers guidance players now receive within the context of their football careers.

Back in my day, I had no idea what was the right decision for my future career and I certainly didn't have all the facts. For instance, I automatically signed with Stoke without finding out if anyone else was interested in me. Years later, I heard that Kenny Dalglish had once tried to sign me for Liverpool but Portsmouth weren't prepared to let me go at the time. Had I known this when my contract at PFC was finished, perhaps I would have approached him. I feel players deserve to know their career options at all times, during their time as professional footballers and after they retire.

Even personal managers and agents shouldn't make the final decision for players. No one has a person's best interests at heart more than they do for themselves. Whenever others enter the debate, there's always an element of vested interest on their part. I've no doubt, now, that Alan Ball was thinking of how well it would reflect on him if he brought his best players up from Portsmouth.

In the end, in life, you're always in the race alone. You have to arm yourself with all the knowledge you can get and then trust that you know best, and that includes being brutally honest with yourself and sometimes making difficult choices. To be successful in life, you need the ability to make decisions even if they are emotionally uncomfortable. You have to manage your own career, whether its football or hairdressing. Similarly, you have to manage your own investments – as I will be pointing out many times through the course of this book.

I have often questioned how well I managed my football career. (Easy to do with hindsight!) While I certainly never lacked passion for the game, I possibly lacked a certain amount of ambition.

For example, during my time at Stoke, Martin O'Neill started managing Leicester. He brought the recently relegated club back from Division One (the renamed second league) to the Premiership (the renamed top league) in 1996. When he first took over at Leicester, he was interested in signing me, but I didn't want to leave Stoke. It could have been my chance to further my career and help put me in contention for the England squad, but I didn't see those opportunities at the time. Although I always had my dream of being a great English football hero, of playing for my country, maybe I never saw it as anything more than a dream.

There's a world of difference between dreams and ambition. By the very nature of the words, an ambition suggests something you believe is achievable, whereas a dream suggests something you consider out of your reach, something intangible and ephemeral. I loved Stoke, I still do. I had the best time there and it's the first club I look out for when I check the football results, but I may have been loyal at the expense of my full potential as a professional footballer.

However, regrets are only negative if no lessons are learned. If you learn something from your decisions that gives you the ability to make better decisions in the future, then you've gained something positive. Instead of a regret, you can call it a learning curve. As Oscar Wilde said, experience is the name everyone gives to their mistakes.

At Stoke under Lou Macari

My loyalty to Stoke wasn't just wrapped up in my loyalty to Alan Ball. In the end, Alan had only lasted a couple of seasons at Stoke City, but I was there for seven years.

Midway through Stoke's first season in the Third Division Alan got the sack and was replaced by Lou Macari, who I struggled to get along with. Lou Macari was very serious; it was all work and no play. He didn't drink and he was a taskmaster. We may have gone back up a division under him, but we never had as much fun as we did under Alan. To be honest, Lou was more the manager I needed, but I was still young when he arrived and resisted his ideas. Many of us did. We just wanted to kick a football around but Lou had us running up hills and doing real physical training. We longed for the old "hard work buys you hard play" days under Alan Ball, but Lou wasn't keen on too much partying going on after hours.

Of course, now I look back, I can see how well Lou treated and managed us players at the time; he was spot on. I hope I get the chance to tell him this some day. I was also probably wise not to follow my old gaffer, my football dad, to his next club... bottom-of-third-division Exeter City.

STOKE CITY, WINNERS OF DIVISION 2, 1992-3

In fact, it was under Lou Macari that I experienced one of the highlights of my entire football career. It was the 1992 Autoglass Trophy (as the Football League Trophy competed for by the third and fourth division teams was then known) final. It was the first time Stoke City had played at Wembley since 1972 and it was like we'd hit the jackpot. I had watched so many FA Cup finals on TV and, like any aspiring professional footballer, it was my dream to play at Wembley.

I will never forget the first glimpse of the famous old Wembley twin towers (that have been since replaced by a huge modern arch) as we approached on the coach. We were well prepared and itching to get out and play.

My uncle had travelled to the UK undercover (as he was still apparently a wanted man) from Australia, and my 80 year-old nan was also in the crowd, along with the rest of my family. As I walked out on to the turf and saw my entire family up in the stands, I had never felt more proud. It was a very emotional moment; I can still get choked up thinking back on it now. It was a close game against Stockport County, but we won 1-0 after a brilliant goal from Mark Stein.

As I walked up with my teammates to get our trophy, I realised I was about to meet a brilliant man I had met once before. Bobby Moore was there to present the winning team with their medals. He was in the bar afterwards and my nan walked straight up to him to tell him how wonderful he was and to thank him for giving her beloved grandson a medal. The image of my nan talking to Bobby Moore seemed almost surreal. It also meant the world to me because throughout my career, the most important part of it has been sharing special moments with my friends and family. Whenever I could get someone down to the changing rooms to meet their sporting heroes, I would.

Later, when the celebrations were dying down, my brother Paul and his mate and I were walking down the side of the pitch and we saw a balloon floating around in front of one of the goals. We ran out on to the pitch and started playing with it. As Paul headed it past me into goal, recreating a Match of the Day moment, I heard one of the Wembley groundsmen shouting at us, "Oi! Get off the pitch!" We felt like we were schoolboys again!

Lou Macari did a great job at Stoke, but after another change in manager (Joe Jordan arrived when Lou went to Celtic), I began to ask myself if it might be time for me to move on too. Around this time, rumours began to surface that there was interest in me at Sheffield United, a club that had recently been relegated to the country's second league (Division One, soon to be renamed the Championship).

After seven seasons and three managers at Stoke City, it was hard to say goodbye, but I was more than ready for a new challenge. I had a number of mates at Sheffield by then, so it felt like the right place to go.

LIFTING THE AUTOGLASS FOOTBALL LEAGUE TROPHY AT WEMBLEY, 1992

CHAPTER FOUR:
EVEN FURTHER NORTH

Signing for Sheffield United

DURING THE 1995-1996 season my great friend Adrian Heath (the ex-Everton midfielder) was appointed assistant manager at Sheffield United under Howard Kendall. One Sunday lunchtime, just as that season was coming to an end, I found myself sitting in the back of a Mercedes with Adrian, in the car park of the country pub a bunch of us used to meet up at, signing a contract.

Back in the days of Sunday opening hours, when pubs were only open from midday until about 2.30pm, they used to get completely packed. We couldn't even find a table, let alone hear ourselves speak, so we ended up sitting in the car while we went over the contract details. That's when I discovered that Stoke had sold me to Sheffield for half a million pounds. I couldn't get my head around being worth that much. It was a good deal for me, my wages were going to be doubled and there were the usual bonuses associated with cup wins and league promotion.

As usual, I negotiated my own deal. Most players used to negotiate their own deals back then, sometimes with the help of a PFA rep, but times were beginning to change, with sports agents becoming more and more prevalent. The hit film *Jerry Maguire*, in which Tom Cruise plays the eponymous über-sports agent, helped to catapult the notion of agents into the sporting zeitgeist when it came out in cinemas early in 1997.

When I arrived at Sheffield United for the 1996-1997 season, I heard that a number of the players, including the great Scottish midfielder, Don Hutchinson, were being represented by a sports agent called Rachel Anderson. Rachel was the UK's only female footballers' agent, and the only woman accredited by FIFA. She approached me and I signed with her, just before she hit the headlines.

Every year, the PFA holds its annual awards dinner at the Grosvenor House hotel in London. It's always a great event, and a chance to catch up with mates from old clubs. That particular year, I was going in a group of footballers from Sheffield and one of the lads had invited our agent, Rachel, to come along as his guest. There was nothing unusual about inviting an agent as a guest, except for the fact that all the other agents were men.

When we arrived, the PFA decided to refuse to admit Rachel on the grounds that she was a woman and it was traditionally a men-only event. The incident caused quite an uproar; the press got wind of it and Rachel got the support of then sports minister Tony Banks as well as the prime minister himself, Tony Blair. She ended up suing the PFA for discrimination. We were all on her side and it was a great victory when she won.

That annual dinner was legendary. Most of us would stay in the same hotel near Hyde Park Corner and after dinner, every year, we would go back and literally drink the bar dry. One year, the Professional Jockeys Association was having its annual dinner at the same hotel so there was double the trouble.

With hindsight, I do feel sorry for the other people who were staying there. If I arrived in a hotel with my family today and saw the place was packed out with loud, boozed-up footballers and jockeys, I think I'd walk straight out again. It makes me cringe now to think what we were like back then!

A difficult start in South Yorkshire

Adjusting to life in Sheffield was harder than I'd bargained for. Stoke had been home for seven years. Now I had to find my way in a new city, at a new club, with new teammates and new fans. I was completely out of my comfort zone. It might have been easier if there hadn't been a huge black cloud hanging over me.

Mum was seriously ill. She'd been diagnosed with the asbestos-related disease, mesothelioma. None of us knew for sure where she had been exposed to asbestos but we began to hear of other cases afflicting some of the people who had worked in the car parts factory where she'd been for years so in the end we assumed that it must have been there.

I'd been told that mum was poorly, but I had no idea how bad it was. Or maybe I hadn't wanted to accept how bad it was. I'm sure there was a little denial going on. I was struggling at Sheffield and I probably couldn't handle the added stress. As an expensive new signing, I was under pressure to perform and I knew I wasn't doing my best. Mentally, I just wasn't there. My mind was on my mum. I also felt a bit lost without my network of friends at Stoke; the people I'd known for most of my adult life were miles away.

ON THE BALL FOR SHEFFIELD UNITED

I knew Sheffield United was a great club and even though we had just been relegated, no one thought that we would stay down for long; there was a real buzz in the air, you could really feel the passion and the potential. It was just tough for me trying to make new friends and impress the coach with so many worries on my mind. I was 28 and separated from my family while they were going through a particularly tough time. I felt guilty not being there. I was also lonely. I was living further from home and further north than I'd ever lived, and I was discovering that the cold really does get into your bones and your brain! In the end, I went to see the manager. I felt I owed it to him, and myself, to tell him what was going on at home.

Howard Kendall was a big cigar aficionado. When you first walked into his office, you would find yourself talking to a disembodied voice for a while, until you made it through the thick clouds of cigar smoke and arrived at the desk.

I sat down and told him all about mum. He was brilliant. He told me I could take whatever time off I needed to go and visit her and be with my family. Strangely, once I got permission to go, I didn't leave. I don't know why. Maybe on a subconscious level I felt if I went down there I would be admitting how bad things were. If I avoided making the trip, I could convince myself that it wasn't that serious, that mum was going to get better.

The months rolled on and, as we approached the end of the season, our chances of being promoted back to the Premiership weren't looking good. We lost Howard Kendall to Everton and Nigel Spackman took over as player-manager.

Nigel and I had signed with Sheffield on the same day at the beginning of the season. We had done all the press conferences together. He was a great player, but there's always a little tension amongst players when one of the team gets promoted to manager, and some dust settling had to take place in the wake of Howard's departure. However, I liked Nigel and I was determined to get off to a good start in his first season.

Things felt more settled with mum, too. When the season had ended, I'd spent some time at home, and mum had even been up to Sheffield to visit me at the start of training. I finally felt some weight lifted off my shoulders and it looked like things were on the up.

Heartbreak

On Tuesday 12 August 1997, I was at the training ground doing some of our usual drills when I noticed a policeman walk up to one of the assistant coaches and start speaking to him. They looked over at me and I knew. I just knew it was mum. I ran over immediately.

The first thing that struck me was how old and traditional the policeman looked. This moment was going to be etched in my memory forever and I remember wishing it could have been a different looking policeman bearing the bad news. I wanted the memory of a younger man, with a kinder face, looking more compassionate. This chap was perfectly nice, but he looked severe. He was old, with grey hair and a stiff moustache. He could have come straight out of an episode of a BBC country drama set in the 1940s... a typical British bobby on the beat, cycling along a country lane, shouting at the schoolboys who were frightening the cows.

Paul had been trying in vain to get hold of me at the club and on my mobile. In a panic, he'd eventually phoned the police and asked them to try and find me. I had to get to Basingstoke immediately. Mum was in a coma.

I showered as fast as I could. I was in a complete daze. My friend David White stayed in the changing rooms with me, offering me friendly support and trying to console me. I was a mess; I couldn't stop crying.

Then I did what every person does (but shouldn't do) when they're in that state of mind: I got into my car and shot down the M1, going at over 100mph all the way. I was in a state of total shock; the tears wouldn't stop pouring down my face. I kept looking at my mobile phone, lying on the seat next to me, willing Paul to call me. I knew he would call if there was a chance I was going to make it to see her. The longer it was silent, the more afraid I became. I didn't want to believe she was gone. I had to believe I was going to make it to say goodbye.

I made it to Basingstoke in record time. I drove through the town centre, jumping every red light I came to; it was a miracle I never got stopped. When I finally pulled up outside the hospice and jumped out of the car, I left the engine running and the door open. But Paul and Dad were waiting for me at the front door, and their faces said it all. I was too late.

She was gone.

I sank to my knees. I was sure I could feel my heart breaking in two inside my chest. I couldn't breathe. I don't remember exactly what happened next. It was like time stopped for a bit. I knew mum was ill, but I didn't think she could just die without due warning. For a long time, I simply couldn't get my head around it.

The next few weeks were a blur. I drove back and forth between Sheffield and Basingstoke, supporting my family, helping to sort mum's affairs out, having the funeral and trying to come to terms with it all. I needed to be there for my dad, who was obviously in pieces.

There is one moment I remember quite clearly. I'd just got off the phone with Nigel, who was pressing me to tell him when I'd be getting back to Sheffield that day, when I turned on the radio. It must have been the morning of Sunday 31 August because it was the moment I first heard the news that Princess Diana had died. The first thing I thought was... now there are two angels in heaven. Somehow that helped.

Mum's death left a huge hole in my heart and I couldn't forgive myself for not being there when she went; it haunted me.

One day, I was driving back to Sheffield after spending a day with my dad in Basingstoke and suddenly I found I was crying so hard I had to pull over. The tears just wouldn't stop flowing and I was shaking from head to foot. Suddenly my phone went. It was my cousin, Dawn, calling from Australia. I knew Dawn was a really successful medium in Australia, but I wasn't sure if I believed in all of that psychic stuff.

"Hello, Lee," she said, in her sing-song Australian twang. "It's Dawn, your cousin, calling from Australia. Listen, love, I just got a message from your mum. She says, everything's all right. She says everything's going to be okay, love." I was stunned. I thanked her and chatted for a short while. When I hung up, I felt a lot better.

I continued to drive up to Sheffield feeling strangely calm, and comforted by Dawn's call. I kept thinking to myself, I mustn't forget her voice. I told myself, over and over, "Don't forget mum's voice," and to this day, if I want to remember mum's voice I just have to go somewhere quiet and listen carefully. I always manage to hear her clearly. She's calling up to my bedroom in our old house, saying, "Lee! Turn your music down!"

CHAPTER FIVE:
STICKING MY NECK OUT

FA Cup semi-final

THE BEGINNING OF the following season at Sheffield was one of the toughest times of my life. I felt extremely guilty being so far away from home and, in particular, from my dad. I was still shaken up over the loss of mum and I couldn't seem to get back on form.

The mood at the club didn't help. Everyone was a bit low after we'd failed to get promoted, and Nigel was pushing us harder than ever. He ended up leaving before the end of the season and Steve Thompson (Tommo) became our caretaker manager for a short while.

Tommo managed to pick our spirits up right from the minute he took over. He was like a light in a storm. I was happy because I knew Tommo liked me. Even though it looked like we were going to miss out on promotion again, we were doing well in the final knockout rounds of the FA Cup. We beat Coventry at home at Bramall Lane in an exciting game that went to penalties to reach the semi-finals.

Our semi-final game was against Newcastle. It was due to be held at Old Trafford, at the end of April 1998, a couple of days after my 30th birthday. The game was going to be broadcast live on Sky so the pressure was on.

We were all buzzing with the knowledge that we were one game away from playing in the final at Wembley. Tommo gave us his famous speech in the changing rooms, minutes before we went out on to the pitch. His pre-game pep talks were some of the best I ever heard and he finished up by saying, "Remember, lads, you're only 90 minutes away from *immortality*."

I was marking Alan Shearer, who scored the one and only goal in the match to win the semi-final for Newcastle and put us out of the competition. It was a great game and we came away knowing we'd put in a first-rate performance. I'd had a close shave, though, and had been lucky to finish the game. I brought Shearer down in a messy tackle when I already had one yellow card. Luckily the referee was a bit old school and let it slip. I'm sure the same tackle would be an automatic booking these days! Years later I ran into Alan Shearer while we were on holiday in the same resort in Barbados. We had a nice chat about that memorable game.

The following season, the managerial merry-go-round continued. Steve Bruce took the reins for a season, and then my old mate, Adrian Heath, took over. As we headed further down the league table and towards the relegation zone of the Championship the following season, it looked like Adrian's days were numbered, too. Then, finally, in 1999, Neil Warnock arrived at his home club to begin what eventually became an eight-year managerial stint, which culminated in the club's promotion back to the Premier League in 2006.

For me, Neil's arrival seemed to bring with it a sense of stability. He was a local Sheffield lad and a lifelong Blades supporter. He brought Kevin Blackwell with him, who was a great assistant manager. Then Keith Curle transferred from Wolves where he'd had a frustrating couple of seasons while the club struggled for promotion. Keith was approaching the end of his playing career and Neil was prepping him for a coaching position.

It had been a rough few years in the aftermath of mum's death, but now I tentatively started to believe that the worst was over, that things were on the up. I did have a couple of really good seasons under Neil Warnock... until life went and dealt me another huge blow.

Serious injury

One afternoon in March 2001, I was doing some heading practice in training. The assistant coach was driving some pretty hard balls at me, from 50 yards back, and I remember my neck was feeling a bit tired. At one point, as I went to head the ball, I felt a painful twinge in my neck. It didn't impede my movement too much and I assumed I was in for a bit of a stiff neck for a few days. As a defender, I regularly suffered from slight neck strain, and I'd had back problems on and off throughout my career. My initial thought was that it was nothing new, but this turned out not to be the case.

The following week, we were playing an evening game, under floodlights, at Bramall Lane. We hadn't been playing long when I went to intercept the ball, in front of one of the opposition's strikers, with a header. As I jumped up to head the ball, I felt something snap inside my neck.

What it actually felt like was as if my whole head was about to detach and shoot off my body, as if there was nothing holding my head onto my neck. It was the most excruciating pain I had ever felt. I collapsed on the pitch and had to be taken off immediately. Apparently I was as white as a ghost. I was rushed to hospital for MRI scans. At first I couldn't even lie down in the scanner, the pain was so intense.

In the following days I had several consultations with specialists. None of them had good news, with one actually suggesting that the only solution was to insert a piece of plastic in my neck. This would have prevented any side-to-side movement of my neck, effectively ending my career on the spot. Finally, Nigel Cox, our fantastic physiotherapist at the time, decided we were going to get an opinion from a new specialist in Birmingham he'd just heard about, Andre Jackowski. Nigel's decision bought me a few more years playing football and saved me from a seriously reduced quality of life.

Andre Jackowski had operated on Aston Villa's Dion Dublin after a particularly nasty collision left him with a broken neck. Dion was back on the pitch just three months after Jackowski had treated him. Nigel and I went to see Jackowski who said he could definitely fix my problem.

He told us he needed to operate immediately to remove some bone that was pressing on my nerves. He said if the operation went well, I would probably make a full recovery.

In order to get to the right place inside my neck, from the right angle, Jackowski had to open up the front of my neck. This left me looking like Frankenstein, with eighteen staples running across my throat. I looked like I had narrowly survived a beheading and I still have the scar to this day. Jackowski proved himself a genius because after only six weeks I was right as rain and playing again.

Before we knew the full outcome of my operation, while I was still in rehab, Neil Warnock approached me to see if I'd be interested in a coaching position. I had my coaching qualification and it seemed a logical future step, but in my compromised state of convalescence, it felt like defeat. I was determined to play again. I wasn't ready to throw in the towel. I had to believe I was going to recover and play again, and that I had a good few years of playing left in me, so I turned him down. When I made my full recovery and found myself back out on the pitch I was glad I had rejected the offer.

When I did return to playing, however, it soon became clear that I wasn't anywhere near my best. I may have recovered physically, but my confidence was completely shot. I would never go for the ball with my head the way I used to. I would hold back. I had become too conscious of the fragility of my neck. I was aware of how lucky I'd been to recover from one injury. I wasn't conscious of trying to protect myself; it was as if my body did it automatically, as if it wasn't prepared to risk my neck again.

Neil didn't say much to me directly but I think we all knew the writing was on the wall. My contract with Sheffield finished at the end of that season and I was starting to worry about whether I had a future there. So it was a great relief when my old school friend Matt called.

A stint at Woking

After a good playing career with Wycombe Wanderers, Matt had taken up the assistant managerial reins at conference club, Woking. He asked if I'd be interested in playing a few games for them. It sounded like a great idea to me. I thought it would give me a chance to get my confidence back, to get myself mentally strong again. However, it was a disaster.

I hated playing at that level. I'd been a professional footballer all my life. I'd been playing in the top three national leagues since the day I turned 16. Suddenly I was playing in a non-league club. Of course I respected my teammates as any professional does – they were a great bunch of lads and we had a good laugh together after games – but I couldn't play at that level. It didn't feel like a professional game. It was a different mindset. Furthermore, Woking FC was in so much financial trouble it was close to administration and that was dampening the atmosphere.

As the season progressed, we started winning a few games and we were creeping up towards the top of our conference division. Then Glenn Cockerill took over as manager. He wanted to bring his own players with him so most of us were dropped. With that I decided to retire. So that's how my professional career ended. After I was dropped from an amateur club! It couldn't have been a bigger anticlimax.

In my youth, when I was at the peak of my career, I imagined how, one day, I would have to retire. I pictured the papers, with the headline of the sports section reading something like, "A Great Loss To British Football As Lee Sandford Retires." I imagined there would be a short announcement on the News at Ten. In my mind I saw a big party, with speeches and plenty of champagne, even a few tears being shed.

What actually happened was, I phoned my dad and said, "Dad, I just retired from football," and then I went down to the pub with Matt and some of the other lads for a couple of beers. I was 34 years old.

Reflecting on my career

I think I was a good professional footballer. I always showed up on time and worked hard. I didn't mess around or cause any trouble. I was the PFA rep for a while at Sheffield United. I had respect for my union and was honoured to hold that position of responsibility.

I always gave my best. I couldn't walk out on to a pitch and not give it my all and I think every manager knew that about me. Aside from some obvious slight dips in form after losing mum, I never let my feelings or emotions get in the way of me putting in my best performance. Even if I wasn't seeing eye to eye with my manager, I would still deliver.

A few years after I retired, I heard Neil Warnock being interviewed on talkSPORT radio about some of the players he'd managed at Sheffield. He mentioned me and praised my consistency. He said that he always knew what he was going to get from me. He compared this to how frustrated he sometimes got with foreign players who struggled to perform in adverse British weather. He knew he could put me out on the pitch and, come rain or shine, he'd get what he expected out of me.

I found I needed a complete break from football once I retired – I couldn't even bear to watch a game or look at the scores. I felt like I never, ever wanted to see a football again. Freddie Flintoff talked of a similar feeling when he retired from cricket, saying that he never wanted to see a cricket ball again. And, of course, Sir Steve Redgrave famously said, "If you ever see me anywhere near a boat again, you have permission to shoot me," when he retired for the first time after winning his fourth gold medal in Atlanta in 1996. (Thankfully no one did because he came back to win his fifth gold in Sydney in 2000!) That's exactly how I felt; I had to take a complete break. Football had consumed me and I needed to do something completely different for a while.

In May 2012, Michael Vaughan made a documentary for the BBC called *Sporting Heroes: After the Final Whistle* in which he interviewed a number of veteran stars from the world of sport, including John McEnroe, Matthew Hoggard, George Foreman and Tony Adams. He asked them how they felt about retirement, about the sense of loss that many sportspeople say they suffer when they retire. Most do feel a sense of loss; although some find they just can't break away from it. For instance, George Forman said, "You need someone to tell you: enough is enough. Most boxers can't find that person. There's always that one punch you think you can land. I think I'll be sitting there at 70 thinking: 'I got one more fight'."

Personally, I identify more closely with Tony Adams who said, "Do I miss the game? No, I don't miss it. Maybe because I don't feel unfulfilled. If I thought I was just Tony Adams the footballer, then it's over." I always knew I wasn't just Lee Sandford the footballer. I was lucky, I always had people around to remind me I was a son, and a father, and a brother, before anything else.

When I look back at my football career, I do look back with pride. I don't know if it was what it *could* have been, or what it *should* have been, but it was a good, solid career that spanned 18 years, with long stretches at three decent clubs. I didn't make it into England's senior squad, but I still played *for* England.

Not only did I play for my country at youth level, but I also played for some of England's best football fans at Portsmouth, Stoke and Sheffield United. I played for English clubs that are over 100 years old. I played over 500 professional games. I'd faced the death of my beloved mum, and a potentially crippling neck injury, and I'd carried on.

Yes, I am proud of my football years.

No longer putting football first

Professional football is a career that consumes you. It has to. You couldn't do it otherwise; you wouldn't last. Someone else would be more dedicated than you and would take your place. It has to be your number one priority. I'm sure that's the reason I never settled down before I retired. I knew I could never put a young family through all of the drama and pressure that a professional football career requires.

In the end, it wears you down, all the constant training and travelling. I longed to eat normally again and to relax on the fitness routine for a while. I wanted to spend a Christmas night at home instead of in a hotel preparing for the Boxing Day game. I wanted to go out with my mates on New Year's Eve and be *normal* for a while.

Mum's death had a lasting impact on me. It had shown me how fragile life is, how the people you love can be here today and gone tomorrow. I wanted to spend time with my family, with Chloe, and dad, and Paul and his family. I was also ready to meet someone to settle down with so I could start a young family of my own.

My family's security has always been incredibly important to me. Security isn't just about money; it's about being there for important events, for birthdays, weddings and graduations. You can't always be there when you're a professional footballer. I knew I was ready to retire because I wasn't prepared to put my family in second place anymore. Football was the reason I wasn't there to say goodbye to mum. On some level I was still getting over that. On some level I probably still am.

I still sometimes wonder if I would ever go back to football, as a career. In my final years as a player I had contemplated, on and off, going into coaching. I had my degree in sports science; I'd done some UEFA coaching badges and some business management courses. I probably could have got myself a half-decent coaching job, but my heart wasn't in it anymore. I needed to put it all behind me for a while. Mum's death, my injury, my loss of form; it was all wrapped up in football and I needed a clean break.

Would I go back to football now, as a coach? I doubt it. Even if for no other reason than how hard it would be to get back into the game. It's such a watertight business now and I know I would have to take a massive step back and get in at a very low level in order to work my way up. I think I missed my entry point when I turned down Neil Warnock's offer of a coaching position after my neck injury. But I could never say *never*.

A new start

I was only in my mid-30s when I retired. I needed a new career.

Fortunately, I'd been investing in property for a while. The properties in and around Stoke that I'd been managing had been doing quite well, so I already had a sort of second career ready and waiting for me. I'd also been dabbling in the stock market for several years and that really fascinated me. I wanted to spend time learning more about trading stocks and shares. It felt like that might be an area in which I could build a new career.

CHAPTER SIX:
TRADING UP

The value of things

I'M NOT SURE exactly how old I was when I first became aware of money and the value of things, but the general notion of material wealth must have made an impression on me at some point.

I knew our house in Basingstoke was better than our accommodation in London. Not only did I have my own bed, I also had my own room; it was a far cry from living over the pub or squeezing into my nan's house. But I don't think I compared it to, say, a six-bedroom electric-gated mansion up the road. I probably wasn't even aware that bigger houses existed. If I had been, I'm sure I wouldn't have cared. As far as I was concerned, we had everything we needed. We were doing okay. I didn't covet anything.

If you're raised by parents who don't go on about wanting more, and you have a safe and warm place to sleep and enough food on the table, and good friends to play with, what else can a young kid desire? (Remember I was growing up in the 1970s, in a time before mass advertising on 24-hour, multi-channel TV.)

If there was a particular moment when I became aware that perhaps some people had more money than us, it was probably when I first went in Matt's dad's car. I knew it was better than my dad's car. Our cars were always old and a bit battered. Dad usually bought them at auction and half the time a window didn't roll down all the way, or the wing mirror was slightly cracked. Matt's dad had a new, fancy car in which everything worked, and all the controls looked very shiny and modern. It didn't bother me, as such. It didn't make me *want* a bigger or better car; it was just an observation.

Then I remember when Matt's dad suggested the whole football team go on a tour to the US with our families. Even with the cost of the flights, hotels and internal transfers at a discounted group rate, mum and dad felt it was going to work out to be too expensive for us all to go. Instead they promised to take Paul and me on our own holiday. They saved and saved, and finally we went with the whole family – uncles, aunts and cousins – on a package holiday to Florida. I remember we flew on Laker Airways, Freddie Laker's original low-cost airline that was the precursor to the likes of easyJet and Ryanair.

We had a brilliant time. We did Disney World and all the other attractions. It's still one of the best memories of my childhood. It showed me, for the first time, the payoffs of hard work. I clearly remember how hard mum and dad worked to save up for that trip. They both took extra shifts and as much overtime as they could get. It was great to see them enjoy the fruits of their labours in the end. It set a great example to my brother and me about how important it is to work hard for your rewards.

I started earning my own money at the age of 16, when I joined Portsmouth as an apprentice. To date, I have never had any particular money worries; at least not on the scale that I now know some people have. In fact, when I was a young lad I wasn't even aware that people *had* money worries – I assumed everyone could get a job whenever they wanted one.

My salary as a footballer may have started small, but it increased rapidly. As a result, I always spent money freely. No one talked to us young footballers about saving or investing some of the money we were earning, so I just bought whatever I needed with the money I had.

It all got very material very quickly in the early 1980s. Thatcher's children were sharp-dressed, BMW-driving, Dirty Dancers. It was all about the suit, the moves and deciding whether you were VHS or

Betamax. I shudder to think how many designer suits I owned by the time I turned 21 in 1989. There were definitely threads by Hugo Boss, Armani, Versace and the like; it was the Miami Vice effect.

Luckily I had the sense to put some of my money in property, even if, at the time, I was just concerned with having somewhere nice to live as opposed to thinking of it in terms of an investment. I bought my first flat in Southsea when I was 18. I never decorated it or bought much furniture, and I can't even recall what the kitchen looked like because I was never in it. I had a nice TV and a stereo and a comfy bed, and that's all I needed. All I cared about was playing football; everything else was gravy.

Two years later, I traded in the flat for a three-bedroom semi-detached house with a long driveway where I parked both my cars. Cars were a bit of a weakness for me back then. I already had a perfectly good car, but one day I was walking past an Audi showroom and I saw something I liked, so I bought it. That's the kind of money I had and that's the kind of attitude I had to spending it.

Around £5 a week went into my PFA pension, but that was it; the rest of my salary I treated like disposable income. In my early 20s, I couldn't imagine my football career ever coming to an end, so I assumed I'd always have plenty of money. I never got into debt, but with the knowledge I have now, I cringe to think about how I threw my money around, about how much I would have now if I'd saved and invested some of it.

I wasn't a Champagne Charlie; beer was always my drink, and maybe a nice bottle of wine with a good meal. I was also lucky that drugs never appealed to me. They were offered, but I never felt the urge to try them. Neither did I get into the gambling bug that I saw some footballers fall victim to. In addition to being drawn to cars and property, I've always had a weakness for luxury travel and holidays. Being pampered in an exotic location is my idea of heaven, and the way I would always choose to wind down and switch off.

I really enjoyed the ability to be generous towards my friends and family.

Again, I tried not to be too flashy, but I'd pick up the drinks tab when I was out with friends, or I'd take my family out to a nice restaurant.

I probably could have given mum and dad more, but they never asked, and I never considered whether they needed it. I was a bit naïve about the true cost of things and what their salaries must have been. Mum used to joke that one day I'd be rich enough to buy her a lovely house in the countryside where she could retire, but it always seemed so far off. I couldn't imagine her at retirement age. When you're young you can only imagine your parents doing exactly what they've always done, living exactly where they've always lived. The thought of change doesn't really cross your mind. Which is why it's such a shock when things do suddenly, and irreversibly, change.

My parents were great role models for Paul and me, and I'm sure they were pleased to see their kids do well. Paul carved out a great career for himself in IT at a time when that sector was booming. He's a successful businessman to this day. We both benefited from the solid support and unconditional love that mum and dad always gave us, and we were inspired by how hard they worked throughout their lives. They also instilled in us the belief that family is everything, that the most important thing you can have is a loving family around you.

I knew family was the one thing that money couldn't buy and I longed to find the right person to settle down with, and start a family of my own with. My lifestyle as a footballer was not conducive to family life – I'd already experienced how hard it was to be a significant part of Chloe's life, living miles away with such a busy training and playing schedule – so I knew I'd probably have to wait until my career started winding down before I settled down properly. (It didn't stop me keeping an eye out for Miss Right though!)

I was also aware that I probably wasn't ready, emotionally, for that kind of commitment. I watched many friends meet girls and get married when they were far too young to know what they wanted. A lot of those marriages ended up in divorce. I definitely didn't want that. When I made the commitment of marriage, it had to be for life. I doubted I'd find the right girl while I was living the typical life of a single professional football. So I was a real nomad for a while.

When I first moved up to Stoke I was only 21 – effectively still a kid. I didn't even think about getting a house for a while and for the first three months I just lived in a hotel. I became great friends with the executive chef. I would come back after training, eat whatever he served up, and we would chat about our days and what was going on in the world. He was an excellent wife for a while, that executive chef! In the end I did buy a little bachelor pad. It was a nice two-bedroom house that was perfectly adequate, and where I lived for a number of years.

If there was one spending bug I did get bitten by, it was the house-buying one. I woke up one morning and just decided, on a whim, to go house shopping; in the same way normal people might wake up and decide to go furniture shopping.

That day I literally walked down to the estate agents, went to see a couple of places and bought one for £179,000 there and then. In the mid-1990s, what I got for that price tag was a four-bedroom, detached house surrounded by a large garden, with two garages and a big sweeping drive leading up to it. It was an unnecessary amount of space for one guy, and I rattled around in that house, living between two rooms, the lounge and my bedroom, wondering why on earth I'd bought such a big house. It was a few years before the late-90s property boom kicked off, so it wasn't the worst decision I'd ever made, financially speaking.

When shopping for property I got a real buzz, and I began to see the potential in owning and managing rental properties. So I started shopping around and ended up buying a few more places in Stoke. The rental income was nice, until I discovered that the stress of having tenants meant you had to put in a lot of effort to earn that income.

Learning about myself

I started investing in property around the same time I was doing my degree, when I was in my first serious relationship with the older woman who owned the health club, and was winding down from the drinking and partying of my youth. These factors combined to give me a real hunger for new knowledge, and this led me to a fascination with psychology. So I ended up going to see a psychotherapist for a few years.

It was strange because I didn't feel I had any specific problems to talk about, but I was on a learning train and I wanted to expand my knowledge of anything and everything I could, including myself. I believed this was the best way of realising my full potential.

He was a great guy, my shrink. He was a big football fan. We talked loads about my childhood and my playing career. I'm sure, in the end, he helped me overcome some old insecurities and build new confidence. The experience consolidated my belief that really knowing yourself inside out is the biggest key to success in life.

The experience also helped to pique my interest in sports psychology. As I was coming to the end of my degree at Manchester, my tutor strongly urged me to specialise in sports psychology and go into the field as a professional. He felt it would be unique to have a sports psychologist who had not only had the academic qualifications, but who had also had so much practical experience as a professional sportsman.

The idea of helping people get the best out of themselves was definitely attractive, and perhaps this was the first hint that I was going to teach one day. But I wasn't sure, even then, whether I wanted to narrow my focus to football. This may also have played a part in me turning down Neil Warnock's offer of a coaching position when I was recovering from my neck injury.

I soon became aware that I had a real interest in money. Not just earning money, but how money worked. Money had always come so easy to me. Footballers are paid a small fortune at the top level. Not only do you get a weekly salary, but you can also get bonuses. Strikers have the incentive of goal bonuses and defenders can help earn the team a clean sheet bonus if no goals are conceded.

Plus you get a fee for every appearance you make. For every game that I played for Sheffield United, I got a £1000 bonus fee. If I was a substitute one week and the game was coming to an end, I'd be hovering around hoping to be told to warm up because I was going on. I could be on the pitch for a few seconds before the final whistle blew and I'd still earn that £1000 bonus.

No wonder I never had money worries, no wonder I've never known what the price of a gallon of petrol is, or how much a pint of milk or loaf of bread costs! I don't take any of it for granted; I know now how lucky I am that I've never been broke, that I've never had to worry about money.

The money also allowed me to play around with investing, and learn (sometimes the hard way) what worked and what didn't. This in turn became the early seeds of my future second career.

CHAPTER SEVEN:
TRADING COLLEGE

An introduction to trading

SHORTLY AFTER I bought my first property in Stoke, I was chatting to one of my teammates, Graham Shaw, about money in general and I finally asked him what we'd all been wondering. How come he had a much bigger house than everyone else? We were all on similar salaries but not only did he have a much bigger house than the rest of us, he also seemed to have more money floating around in general. He told me straight out. He traded shares on the stock market. I decided I wanted to learn how to do it too.

At first I was terrible at it. I made some bad investments and lost money. Slowly, though, I got the hang of it and it became a part of my life. I only ever thought of it as a hobby, but it started to make me a nice little pot of extra cash. Throughout my football career, I kept an eye on the stock market and managed some investments. I only did a few transactions a couple of times a month and I found it fun.

What I did in those days was unrecognisable from what trading is like today. There was no internet. There were none of the derivatives or other complex trading vehicles that are now available to everyone. You just bought and sold shares, and the only way you could check their prices was by looking in the newspaper or watching the teletext services on the TV (Ceefax from the BBC and Oracle from ITV). Every time you wanted to buy or sell shares, you had to ring your broker. There were no online banking accounts with automatic transfers. You even got the physical share certificates in the post.

What I was doing back then wasn't professional trading by any stretch of the imagination; it was taking a punt. It wasn't as risky as gambling, because you were unlikely to lose all your money, but it wasn't particularly structured. I never did much research on a company in the way you can these days; back then there was far less visibility anyway, it was harder to obtain information about companies. I wasn't basing my decisions on much more than a few tips from mates and what I read in the news. Reading the *Financial Times* and having a Barclays Bank trading account made me feel quite grown up. Often Graham would tell me what he was buying or selling and I'd follow him; he certainly seemed to know what he was doing.

When I moved to Sheffield, through my continuing interest in the property market, I met a property developer called Ralph. We became great friends. We used to go on skiing holidays together with mutual friends, and we regularly went out to social events in Sheffield.

As well as developing properties, Ralph traded currencies in the forex market. I asked him to teach me what he knew and then I started doing it, too. Eventually, we went on to become business partners. I still had some properties in Stoke but, with Ralph, I also started investing in properties in Sheffield. We'd go to auctions to buy run-down properties then we'd do them up quickly and sell them on for a profit.

Luckily, I offloaded most of my properties by around 2007, ahead of the crash. This was an advantage I got from following the stock markets: I knew what to look for, so I could more or less see when the peaks and troughs of the property market were coming.

While I was still playing football, I never considered trading to be a potential source of income. Football was my job; properties were my investment; trading was my hobby. After dabbling in trading for ten years, I probably made no more than £20,000. I'd got my brother, Paul, into trading as well. He was good at it and also made a little bit of money, but it was always something we did on the side. It was something to chat about. We liked sharing tips and it was exciting when we made a good profit.

When my football career came to an end and I had to think about what I could do next, I realised my hobby had actually become quite a big part of my life. If I had to choose a second career, I decided it would probably have something to do with trading.

In the past, whenever I met new people who didn't know me and who weren't football fans, maybe on holiday or through non-football friends, they would invariably ask what I did for a living. When I said, "I'm a professional footballer," they would often say, "But what do you *really* do." I always found myself wishing I had a second answer. After I retired from football and started trading full-time, I was able to say, "I'm a market trader." They would usually look impressed and then say, "Oh, I've always fancied doing a bit of that myself."

Subsequently, people started coming to me and asking me to teach them how to trade the markets. That's how I discovered my love of teaching. I had never been motivated by money per se, but trading did enable me to keep up the level of income I'd grown accustomed to as a professional footballer. When I discovered I had quite a talent for teaching, I found something that fulfilled me almost as much as playing football had.

Turning pro again

Initially, I remained based in Sheffield after I retired. I'd built up a good life there. I had friends, I was in a relationship and I had some local business interests. So that's where I set up my first office from where I operated as a professional trader. Luckily, trading is a business you can operate from anywhere.

Eventually, my girlfriend at the time was headhunted by a company in London, so we decided to move back down south. I was actually thrilled. It was time for me go back to my roots and be closer to my family. We moved down to Teddington, which is where I've lived ever since. That relationship eventually ran its course, but I'll always be grateful for the fact that it prompted my move back home. It was a good decision.

It turned out that Teddington was the perfect place for me. At the time, I was still suffering from the post-football blues and was repelled by all things related to football. So to find myself living in close proximity to Twickenham – rugby central – was perfect! There were rugby players living on every block and no one cared two hoots about football. For my entire adult life I'd lived where people knew who I was. In Stoke and in Sheffield, I'd bump into fans or people from the club all the time, but in Teddington no one knew me. I was invisible. I went about my daily life without attracting a second glance from anyone. I liked it. I needed it for a while.

I loved my new career. The financial markets fascinated me and I eagerly followed the new developments in online trading. I was also still being approached by people wanting me to teach them how to trade on an increasingly frequent basis, so this led me to the idea of starting a trading college to teach people about trading.

Teaching trading

My initial foray into teaching didn't work out. I tried to jump on board with other people and then discovered we had different ideas and teaching structures. At first it seemed like a good fit. I met a couple of guys who had been running a small company teaching trading. I thought they had all the tools and the structure to market the type of company I wanted to develop, and that I could invest the money to build the business. However, soon after we joined forces I found I wasn't happy with the general philosophy of the company so we parted ways.

Going it alone was a little nerve-wracking at first, but I knew I had to be in control of the integrity of the company, and market it in a way I felt was honest and effective. It clearly worked, because I soon had several happy clients and business began to snowball. The experience taught me that there is much truth in the saying, "If you want something done properly, do it yourself!"

I wanted to build a company that provided resources and a support network for traders, whether they were experienced or completely new to the game. I started out, very small and completely on my own, in December 2009. At first I relied on word of mouth. Most people approached me because they were a friend, or a friend of a friend, or a distant relation, of someone I had taught.

It wasn't a place where people came to learn a skill and then went off and never came back. I found that people wanted to stay in touch on a regular basis and use the resources I was developing for them. It became more than just a place to learn – it was like having a community of traders helping each other grow.

People who came to me began to get good at trading and started to make real money, which in turn helped them to turn their lives around and take control of their finances in a way they'd never thought possible before. It was inspiring watching people develop their lives in this way.

MY NEW PROFESSION AS A TRADING TEACHER

The name I chose for the business was Trading College. This reflected my feeling that trading is a constant learning process. No one has a perfect formula; no trader knows everything there is to know. We are all still learning – I am *definitely* still learning myself! I had seen a gap in the market. The industry needed a company that offered trading education with knowledge and integrity. I was proud when I realised that I was building it.

I continued educating myself while I educated others. As well as reading up on new trading techniques and IT solutions, I studied neuro-linguistic programming (NLP), becoming a qualified practitioner, and I did a course in public speaking with a professional coach. I started to build all these skills into my teaching process to share with others.

As I've said before, making money alone never motivated me, but acquiring new skills that can be applied to trading and life itself, and then sharing those skills with others... that's what gets me out of bed in the mornings.

Working smarter, not harder

When I look back at how hard mum and dad worked all their lives, for a fixed hourly wage, I am stunned to see how diametrically opposite my life is. With a few clicks of a mouse, from anywhere with internet access, I have the opportunity to make several thousands of pounds in a matter of hours. Our lives these days have become about working smarter, not just harder.

I learnt by example. My parents never had to tell me to work hard for a living because I saw them do it. I was then able to take it a step further and increase my working hours-to-income ratio. We came from a working class family and my parents were from the generation who were told how much they could earn based on their qualifications. We took that a step further.

My brother, Paul, often talks about how our children will have "third generation wealth." We succeeded and became wealthy off the back of how hard our parents worked, giving us a good start in life. We were inspired to go out and make a decent living. We exceeded our parents' wealth. Next, our children will have even more benefits, because we can afford to give them greater opportunities and more freedom of choice than their parents and grandparents had before them.

Sometimes it actually bothers me that I'm not out there working a nine to five job. I almost feel guilty about it, like I'm cheating. At least I can give back by helping others. When my number's up and I'm standing at the pearly gates with St. Peter asking me what I did with my life, I don't want to be saying that all I did was take, take, take. I want to be able to say I shared my knowledge with others; that I passed on as much as I could.

I used to think, naïvely, that everyone had similar parents to mine, that everyone's parents set them a good example and supported them, and encouraged them to do their best. However, meeting so many different people from such a variety of backgrounds through the course of teaching has been eye opening. Now I know that not everyone had parents who taught them the value of money, or showed them how to work hard for a living.

Through Trading College, I've met people who've had chronic financial problems. They were not uneducated people; they were intelligent people who had come unstuck as a result of their own decisions. It started to make me wonder if there were unconscious, psychological reasons underlying these cases. Were people somehow self-sabotaging their finances? My long-standing interest in psychology kicked in and I wanted to help people identify the reasons behind why they had messed up their finances.

I was concerned that I couldn't market this because if I offered a course called 'Trading Psychology', I thought I'd get about eight people signing up for it, whereas if I offered a course called 'Learn the Hottest Trading Strategy Ever', I was sure I'd sell out 100 places in an hour. I had to build this element of psychological assessment into my training programme quite subtly. That alone tells you a great deal about most people's attitude to money. People desire the quick, easy fix. Of course money doesn't come that way. It takes hard work, unshakeable patience and watertight discipline.

People come to my seminars complaining about their financial situation, weighed down with money worries. The first thing I try to impress upon them is that complaining about your situation is never going to change anything. If you're lucky enough to live in a free society and you've got even a basic level of intelligence, you can change your situation. That's not to say it's going to come easy; it is going to take hard work and smart work, but you can change things. It is all about psychology and attitude, about what goes on between the ears.

If ever there was a time when people needed to get creative about how they earn a living, it's now. At the time of writing, the global economic situation is still on shaky ground. The job market is unstable; there are no guarantees and few safe career paths.

The advantage of learning how to trade is that it gives you the opportunity to make money outside of a traditional salaried job. Anyone can buy and sell shares, it is a complete meritocracy, and these days you can do it anywhere. You can be sitting at the back of a bus managing your trades on your iPhone. You can be making money while you sleep. There are no more barriers to wealth. If you're prepared to learn, you have access to as much as the next person. The only things that stand in the way of a person's ability to make money from trading is confidence and a willingness to learn.

My favourite students at Trading College, and the ones who usually end up being the most successful traders, are the people who knew nothing about trading when they arrived. That's because they come with a blank page in their mind and are usually willing to accept all the information they are given without questioning it.

The worst people to try and teach are those who have been trading for years. No matter what you try and tell them, they are often stuck in old thought patterns and find it very hard to relearn techniques. Most people are reluctant to learn new skills, let alone relearn skills they believe they already have.

Watching people build their skills as traders, whether they are professionals or doing it as a hobby and hoping to turn it into a full-time career down the line, is the most rewarding part of what I do. I love watching people regain control of their finances, earn additional income and get on the road to financial security.

Importance of family

A few years after moving to Teddington, I met the woman I wanted to settle down with and we started a family together. We are now the proud parents of a gorgeous little girl. The birth of my daughter, Isabelle, completely changed me as a person; her security means everything to me. All I do, all day, is worry about her. I worry about her health, her future, her education. She is the first thing I think about when I wake up and the last thing I think about as I fall asleep. I always knew I wanted a family of my own, but I never imagined exactly how it would feel. I never knew this level of love, or responsibility, before, and it is a huge relief to me that I have the ability to support my family financially.

Anyone with kids will know what I'm talking about and will tell you that it is a weight that never goes away. When I meet people who are struggling to support their own families, I am driven to try and help them. I get an enormous sense of satisfaction when I help people acquire the skills that might enable them to achieve their goals.

Mum and dad taught me that family is everything. I love them so much for that. They supported us and they worked hard their whole lives to provide us with security. Every day, inspired by them, I strive to do the same for mine.

Now, my dad's opinion of me means more to me than anyone's. As long as dad is proud of me, I can deal with all the other ups and downs in life. He gave me a great start in life and I want to make him proud. I think I do, or at least he hasn't told me otherwise so far!

PART TWO

TRADING THE MONEY MARKETS

A basic introduction

I WOULD LIKE to start by establishing exactly what this part of the book *is*, and what it *isn't*.

It is not:

- An instruction manual on how to get rich quick (keep buying lottery tickets).

or

- A guide to choosing long-term investments (call your financial advisor).

It is:

- A basic introduction to trading the money markets.

As with any potential learning curve, you should read on with an open mind.

Maybe you've never even heard of trading the money markets; maybe you've been a trader for years. Either way, start from a neutral point. Even if you think you know everything there is to know about trading, put those preconceptions aside and look at it afresh. If you don't like my approach, you can always go back to your old methodology, so it can't hurt to consider another perspective.

I'm not making any promises. I can't guarantee that by "x" point in time you will make "y" amount of money from trading, mostly because, while I can share my knowledge with you, I can't control what you do with the knowledge; that's your responsibility. However, I can tell you that I earn an income that's more than comfortable to live off by employing the methods and taking the approach that I am about to share with you.

Why am I sharing it all with you? Because I'm a generous guy. Seriously. Why shouldn't I? I don't lose out by sharing my knowledge with you. As I will come on to explain, there isn't a limited pot of money out there, so we're not in competition with each other.

CHAPTER EIGHT:

THE VIRTUAL WORLD OF MONEY

What money is

LET ME ASK you a very simple question. How do you feel about money? What does it mean to you? When you say the word **money**, what are the associations you make in your mind? Sit with that for a while because we are going to come back to it. Now ask yourself if you really understand what money is.

Most money transfers these days are made electronically. Our salaries are deposited electronically, we book our flights online, we pay our bills by direct debit, we pay for our shopping using debit and credit cards. Even when you have actual cash in your hands, it's only a representation of worth. When you hold a £5 note, you are holding a piece of printed paper; it's only worth something because there's an agreement between you and the person you give it to that it's worth a certain amount of money. That amount is guaranteed by the Bank of England, or if it's another currency, by the central bank of the country that issued it.

We live in a world of exchanges and promises – money is not real. It controls our lives and causes us so much anguish because we cannot survive in the modern world without it, but it only really exists in a virtual sense.

The credit trap

I know a couple who met relatively late on in life. They were both in their early 40s when they met and started a relationship and eventually got married. They were highly paid professional people who worked in similar industries in similar roles. They had earned very similar salaries for the 20-odd years they had both been working.

When they met, they both lived in nice flats that they owned, in upmarket parts of London, and they both owned reasonably fancy cars. In fact, they had lived such parallel lives it was a miracle they didn't meet sooner. However, there was one huge difference between them.

Aside from his mortgage, Brian (let's call him) had never been in debt. He had a couple of credit cards, but he'd always paid them off, every month. He had a few investments, a high interest savings account, and he maintained a healthy minimum balance in his current account. He'd always lived like this.

Kate (let's call her) had a mortgage, too. Plus two hefty bank loans secured on it. She had a major credit card and three store cards. All of them had outstanding balances that were always close to their maximum limit. She only ever paid the minimum amount every month. She'd always lived like this. She was always slipping into the overdraft in her current account.

So how do two people, who have earned roughly the same amount of money throughout their lives and lived similar lifestyles, end up in such vastly different situations? How do they end up on different sides of the credit line?

When Kate met Brian and he analysed her finances, she was gobsmacked to discover that their similar lifestyles (in terms of holidays, restaurants and general living costs) had cost her an extra £20,000, because she had paid a whopping £20,000 over the years (an average of £1000 per year) in interest. Her lifestyle, almost identical to Brian's, had cost her an unnecessary extra £20,000. Why? Because she had lived her whole life on the **wrong side of the credit line**.

This is not a modern concept. Charles Dickens was more than aware of the problem. As Mr. Micawber says to David Copperfield:

> "Annual income twenty pounds, annual expenditure nineteen nineteen six, result happiness. Annual income twenty pounds, annual expenditure twenty pounds ought and six, result misery. The blossom is blighted, the leaf is withered, the god of day goes down upon the dreary scene, and, in short, you are for ever floored. As I am!"

We all know we should be earning interest and not paying interest, but the difference between knowing and doing seems to be the undoing of many of us.

Our material lives are made up, mostly, of the things we own. Some of these things **appreciate** in value and some **depreciate** in value. Property, gold, precious stones and works of art by well-known artists are examples of things that are likely to appreciate in value. Cars, clothes, furniture (unless antique) and electrical equipment are examples of things that are likely to depreciate in value. In general, you want to make sure you have plenty of things that appreciate in value and not too many things that depreciate.

Owning a share in a company, or owning an amount of a commodity, is just like owning anything else; only some days it will **appreciate** in value and some days it will **depreciate**. Some days that share, or commodity, will behave like a house and some days it will behave like a car. Ideally, you want to buy that share after it has been behaving like a car for a certain period of time, and sell it after it has been behaving like a house for a period of time.

However, you are not limited to buying and selling stocks and shares. And nowadays, you do not even need to own something in order to make money from its price fluctuation.

What can you trade?

When you were a kid, you traded football cards, or stamps and coins, or comics. Now you've grown up, you're still trading, but now you're trading slightly bigger items and with a little more risk.

Everything in life is a trade. If you go to work for someone, you are trading your skills for your salary. When you buy something, you are trading your money for the thing you want to own.

In terms of trading in the money markets, you can buy and sell:

- **Shares in a company**: You can buy shares in a company and aim to sell them when their price goes up, to make a profit.
- **Commodities**: You can buy a quantity of gold, or crude oil, or soya beans one day and sell another day at a better price in order to make a profit.
- **Foreign currencies**: You can buy an amount of one currency with another currency and when the exchange rate moves in your favour, sell it for a profit.
- **Government bonds**: You can own a piece of a nation's debt by buying a government bond at a certain price then selling it on when the value goes up, in order to make a profit.

The problem with all of the above is that, if you physically own these things, you can only make a profit if you manage to sell at a price higher than you bought at. You need the price to keep going up, but there is no guarantee of that happening.

Even when the price of your stock does go up, it doesn't typically go up very quickly. You will likely have to hold onto your stock or commodity, or whatever it is you are trading, for long enough to make a decent profit.

This is **long-term investing**. This is the way people have traditionally made money from trading, but it's not the safe bet it once was. For this reason it makes sense to look at other ways of making money out of market fluctuations too, such as trading **derivatives**.

Derivatives

It is probably true to say that the explosion in derivatives trading following the deregulation of the US finance sector was a major contributor to the global financial crisis. That is why derivatives have bad press. However, until the big bankers and hedge fund managers stop doing it, wouldn't we be a little foolish not to take a piece of the action? If you can't beat them join them.

With derivatives the thing to remember is that it's not real; it's all virtual.

Derivatives are products, or financial instruments, that are literally derived from actual, physical tradable items. The price is derived from an underlying asset or the position of an index, and a contract is made based on the performance of that asset or position. Thus, what you are really doing, when you make a contract based on a derivative, is **betting.** You are making a contract – betting – that the price of an underlying asset will rise or fall in a certain time period. It is not gambling, as I will come on to explain.

There has been real controversy over this type of trading because of the huge risk associated with it. There is a feeling that it is an unethical practice, especially with fund managers not always disclosing their practices to the investors who have entrusted them with their money.

Indeed, much of what brought the banking world to its knees in 2008 is blamed on unregulated derivatives trading, in particular sub-prime mortgage bundles that were not rated accurately by the major rating agencies, making them seem more valuable than they really were.

The bad press may be deserved, but that shouldn't prevent you and other traders who take a sensible approach from using derivatives in your trading today, as long as you know what you are doing. The main method of derivatives trading I use, and the one I focus on in this book, is spread betting.

What is spread betting?

Spread betting is a trading vehicle that enables you to take a position on a market or asset without actually owning the physical underlying asset or shares in the market. Then you speculate as to whether the price of that asset or that market will go up or down. You make or lose money according to that movement. Spread betting allows you to trade in a huge variety of markets. You can trade virtually anything.

The **spread** is the difference between the **buy** price and the **sell** price. If you expect the price of the asset you are betting on to rise, you will go **long** and buy at the buy price. If you think the price will fall, you will go **short** and sell at the sell price. The smaller the difference between the two prices (the smaller the spread) the less the market has to move before you are in profit.

As you don't need to buy the actual asset – you just bet on the movement of the price – you can bet large sums on small movements and make far more money than if you owned the asset. You also only put up an initial deposit for your trade amount on the understanding that the broker is lending you the rest of the money you are betting until you make your profit. It's a form of leveraged trading.

Thus you are also liable to lose a great deal of money if you don't have a watertight risk management system in place. You can easily lose more than you initially bet if you don't put into place the safety nets that will protect you. Many people don't. They lose huge sums of money. This gives spread betting a bad name and makes the spread betting brokers a lot of money.

The money you make from spread betting is tax-free. As you don't ever physically own an asset, you are not subject to any capital gains tax or stamp duty. (This is true at time of writing but could change in the future and your personal tax situation may be uniquely affected by other factors.) You also have none of the usual fees and commissions associated with managing assets on a physical level, because no assets are actually being traded.

Practiced carefully and correctly, spread betting is the ideal way to make money in unpredictable, fluctuating markets, because you can make money regardless of which direction the markets move in. The danger is that there are many risks involved. The majority of this section of the book is about how to avoid those risks, and about how to protect yourself from the pitfalls.

If you learn how to trade using spread betting safely, it can be extremely profitable. As you can place a trade on the value of something going down as well as up, you can effectively underwrite your own life. Say you have a credit card with an outstanding debt on it, or a variable rate mortgage. When interest rates go up, you pay more money. However, you can bet on interest rates rising, so you make money as they go up, thus offsetting the profit against the additional interest you are paying on your debts.

It's like backing the opposing team in a football game. It's win/win. You're happy when your team's winning for the points, but if your team loses you win your bet for a cash return.

Trading time frames

There are three basic time frames you can trade within:

1. **Long-term investing** is about buying assets with the intention of holding them for a long period of time. You earn dividends on the shares and you hope that the shares appreciate in value so that you can sell them at a profit down the line. Long-term investors use **fundamental analysis**. They look at the size of the company, its market capitalisation, and its potential for growth. They consider the management structure, the company's mergers and acquisitions policy, and other factors that might affect its value and performance.

2. **Swing trading** is about buying and selling products reasonably quickly in order to make small, short-term profits. Swing traders use **technical analysis**. They use charts to identify trends and range-bound markets.

3. **Day trading** is swing trading at a faster pace. Day traders also use technical analysis, but instead of looking at daily charts, they are looking at hourly charts, or sometimes even five-minute charts, to catch the smallest movements in price. Day trading is not for the faint hearted and only experienced swing traders should try their hand in this fast-paced environment.

Trading is not gambling

Every year I go to Royal Ascot with my mates with the sole intention of having a fun day out. I take £250 in cash with me. I drink lots of champagne and bet on most of the races. I know nothing about horses – I might chat to some of the trainers and jockeys, but I'm basically betting without any information or strategy. The odds of me winning are never even 50/50, so the odds are always weighted towards me losing my money. I play anyway, because it's fun.

I start the day off by betting on the favourites, and I usually win a little money here and there. As the day goes on, and the champagne keeps flowing, I change my approach and start betting on the outsiders, because the idea of them winning is more exciting. The longer the odds on a horse winning, the more thrilling it is to watch the race. Yes, I'm more likely to lose my money, but I'm paying for that adrenalin rush of how much I stand to win if my long shot wins the race. I never come away with any money, I always lose my whole pot, but I always have a great day out with the lads.

That's gambling. There is no risk management, no strategy, no plan, and I change the way I bet halfway through the day.

Some people do trade the financial markets like this, sometimes with huge amounts of money, and sometimes they will make a killing. But they will have been *lucky*. Most people who trade like this will lose. It's not an advisable way to trade unless you have money to burn. Even then, it seems a bit wasteful to gamble when you can easily **bet strategically**.

When I'm trading I have a plan and a risk management strategy. I follow a structure and I study charts that are based on backtesting countless results. Part of my strategy is based on my acceptance that I can't win every time but, unlike horse races, I can work the odds in my favour by sticking to my strategy over the long term.

A successful, professional trader actually does the opposite of a gambler. A smart trader sticks to a specific strategy; a smart trader applies risk management; a smart trader looks to achieve a steadily rising equity curve, rather than sudden big windfalls and losses. We can only control certain factors. We are never in control of what the markets do, but we are always in control of managing our trades.

When you gamble, you place a bet on the outcome of an event. You place your bet at certain odds. If the outcome (the score in a football match, a horse winning a race, snow before Christmas) is what you predicted, you win your money back plus the multiple of the odds you were given. If the outcome is not what you predicted, you lose every penny.

When you are spread betting the money markets, you can put certain safety nets in place to ensure you do not lose all your money. You might lose some money on certain trades, but if you are sticking to a proven trading plan you are also statistically likely to have several winning trades.

Gambling is about sometimes putting "everything on red" – you have a 50/50 chance of doubling your money or losing the lot. Strategic spread betting is about limiting your exposure; you only expose a small percentage of your total pot at any one time. The goal is to ensure you have a steady equity curve. So you could lose 2% of your pot on two trades but make 10% on one trade and therefore still end up in profit.

Derivatives trading is open to you

Some people think derivatives trading is morally reprehensible because these traders are not actually creating anything, they are making money from the daily fluctuations in the global economy.

Maybe it is reprehensible, and maybe a complete overhaul and a strict reregulating of the financial industry is needed. Until that happens, this is the way the big bankers are making money, and it has an adverse affect on traditional investing. If you're happy to have your investments impacted by this practice, fine, but why let them take all the best land and harvest the healthiest crops while you're struggling to put food on the table?

Derivatives trading is open to you, too. Once again though, I must stress that spread betting on derivatives is not an easy game. Practised without proper precautions and education, it will more than likely burn a huge hole in your pocket. It takes some training to get it right. But it is not as complicated as the fancy bankers would have you believe. You don't need a degree and you don't need an expensive suit.

Remember... if I can do it, *anyone* can!

CHAPTER NINE:

YOUR RELATIONSHIP WITH MONEY

Severing emotional ties

COMING BACK TO that question I asked you earlier: how do you feel about money? What is your relationship with money? Do you love it? Do you hate it? Does it scare you? Do you have a love-hate thing going on? Whatever your answer to these questions, they are all wrong, because you *should not have an emotional relationship with money*. Lots of us do, of course.

We need to sever those emotional ties as soon as possible. You will never be able to make good decisions about money if your emotions are always coming into play. Maybe you harbour guilt over a bad investment, maybe you can't get your father's voice out of your head telling you that you were wasteful with money, maybe money worries drove a member of your family to drink. Whatever your old history with money, you need to let go of it before you start trading, or you will be hampered by irrational pressures.

Of course it's not easy. Letting go of the emotions associated with your past experiences is a painstaking process. Your past experiences anchor you, they tell you who you are, they define you; without them, you would feel lost. But there's a difference between acknowledging your experiences and letting their effects limit you. To some degree, you need to reprogram your brain. You need to stop being a victim of your experiences.

Let's do an exercise to help you with this.

Money experiences

Take a piece of paper and write down every bad experience you've ever had regarding money. No one is going to see it, so it doesn't matter how embarrassing or soul-destroying some of them were, just write everything down.

Maybe there are experiences you've never shared with anyone; it's even more important that you write these down. Include decisions that you have made, as well as what you have observed in, and experienced at the hands of, other people. Take your time; get everything down. Come back to it later if necessary.

Don't be scared. Remember, everyone has skeletons in their closet. It actually takes an incredibly strong mind, a particularly sheltered and privileged upbringing, and a lot of good luck not to make some bad financial decisions in your life.

Here's a fictional list, to give you some ideas in case you're struggling:

- When I was 18, I blew the money I'd saved towards buying a car to go on holiday with my friends.
- Mum always said our rich cousins were spoilt, horrible people because they had too much money.
- Grandpa left me £2000 in his will when I was 21 and I invested in my friend's start-up internet company, and lost it all.
- When my girlfriend broke up with me, I sold my flat and went travelling and fell off the property ladder.
- When mum and dad got divorced, they seemed to care more about money than me, which made me hate money.
- I was hopeless at maths at school. I don't understand figures. I glaze over when people talk about interest rates. Money confuses me.
- I'm a shopaholic. I've always had debt problems. I'm a sucker for the store card trap. If I'm offered credit, I'll take it.

How are you getting on? Did you get a few things written down? Good. Now write down all the things you were too scared or embarrassed to write down. GO ON! No one is going to see it. I assure you. Search the memory bank. Leave no stone unturned. When you've finished your list, take a good look at it.

What you're actually looking at is a list of things with which you judge yourself. It's a list of excuses as to why you haven't succeeded where you'd hoped to, of what's held you back from achieving your full potential.

No one judges us more harshly than we judge ourselves. Most of us would never dream of saying the kind of awful things we say internally to another person. Why do we beat ourselves up so much? In his book *Are You Ready To Succeed?* Srikumar Rao calls this inner voice the *voice of judgement*.

Okay, now I want you to take this piece of paper and tear it up.

Really rip it up, into tiny pieces. As you are doing so, forgive yourself. Forgive your parents, forgive your bitchy maths teacher, forgive your spoilt brat cousins, and start afresh. The experiences you have just ripped up are no longer going to affect the way you behave today. You are now a blank slate. You can learn anything. You are capable of making excellent financial decisions.

Remember this process. Remember how it feels, because you are going to do it again, mentally, on a daily basis.

You've just cleaned up your brain computer. You've got rid of old software packages and you're ready to install the new ones, the latest versions.

When you start trading you can't afford to judge your choices as being good decisions or bad decisions or you will build up more emotional reactions that will affect future decisions. You will simply have more profitable days and less profitable days.

When your portfolio is down for a day or so, you are only lending money to the markets. As long as you are still in open trades, you could get that money back the next day. You haven't actually lost money until the trade has been closed out at an actual loss.

Taking control of money

So why should you learn how to trade and take all this control over your money? Because times have changed and we've discovered that the people we once trusted have not always looked after our best interests.

Back in the day, everyone had a personal bank manager, usually the same one for long period of time, not a different one every six months. You would talk through your investments with your bank manager and get their advice; you would trust them. These days, you are more likely to get a kid straight out of college who is only interested in the commission he gets for selling you the bank's financial products, or in pushing credit cards at you, tempting you into debt.

There's a huge amount of temptation out there. Who can blame us for wanting so many material things when they are pushed in our faces on a daily basis through advertising? It's not just our greed that is to blame. The advertisers want us to buy their products, the banks want us to buy their products; everyone is exploiting our natural propensity towards greed and impatience. They've wielded a huge amount of power over us for a very long time. It's time we took some of the power back!

In the not-so-distant past, if you invested in a mutual fund you could trust it would be a safe investment – that you would get your money back with interest. But fund managers, like the rest of us, are prone to greed and impatience themselves. They started making bad decisions with investors' money, and lost a great deal of it. You can no longer rely on other people to make good financial decisions about your money. You need to learn how to make good decisions yourself.

Doesn't it now seem a little crazy to hand over our money to other people to invest for us? Why would they be particularly careful with it? They make their salaries and bonuses regardless. They just make more if they make good decisions with our money. You can't expect anyone else to make a living for you.

It used to be that we didn't have access to the kind of products that bankers were trading, but these days we can more or less do whatever they have the ability to do. Why wouldn't we learn to do it, to become our own investment fund manager and be in control of our own money? I'm sure anyone who invested with Bernie Madoff would advise us to do that now.

We've been lazy. We let go of the reins. We need to take them back. We need to review what our responsibilities are; we need to set a better example to our children.

The first step on the road to taking back control of your finances is to make a plan. People are very good at knowing what they need to do and why they need to do it, but not how it is going to be achieved. Every January there is a huge surge of people signing up for gym memberships but most of them will go to the gym around three times before quitting. The biggest reason they quit is that they haven't made a plan. They know why they need to go to the gym, they've identified that they've stuffed their faces over Christmas and now need to lose weight, but they haven't set out, on paper, how they are going to achieve it. Writing out a plan makes it more likely that they will achieve their goals.

Any successful person will tell you that there is a tried and tested method to achieving your goals. You set your goals, you make a plan, and then you follow it... without quitting. As I've said before, quitting is easy. It's the easiest thing in the world to give up. The harder path is to continue following your plan, even when the going gets tough.

When it comes to trading, 60% of traders don't have a plan and 20% have a plan but don't follow it. The rest are making money. Before I give you some tips on making a trading plan, in the next chapter we'll look at what items and skills you need in your toolbox before you start trading. What are the essential *trading tools*?

CHAPTER TEN:
TRADING TOOL KIT

IF YOU WANT to set yourself up as a swing trader and start spread betting, you need a few basic tools. Some are physical and some are mental. You will need:

1. A computer
2. An internet connection
3. A trading account and broker
4. A pot of money to start trading with
5. A chart package
6. Time
7. Patience
8. Discipline
9. An open mind and willingness to learn, and, of course...
10. Your trading plan.

1. A computer

It's important to have your own desktop or laptop computer. Don't rely on your computer at work; your boss won't appreciate it if he or she catches you managing your trades in the middle of the day, and to begin with you need to be able to do some work over the weekend, setting up trades for the following week.

You may have a smartphone, and that's great for quick checks once you've got the hang of things, but when you're starting out you really need to be able to look at all the information on a proper screen.

2. An internet connection

It amazes me, but I still meet people who don't have an internet connection at home. They're "stealing" it from the flat downstairs, or hopping between cafés with free Wi-Fi. Don't do it! You need a secure and reliable connection so you can check on your trades at any time.

If you're not already internet savvy, take some lessons and get more familiar before you start doing any online trading. You will be placing your trades via the internet, and you need to be able to follow the markets and download your charts.

3. A trading account and broker

You can open a traditional trading account with your bank, or you can open a share dealing account online, such as with Barclays Stock Brokers (**www.barclaysstockbrokers.co.uk**). Or you can go with a specialist online spread betting broker.

If you Google "spread betting brokers" you will be inundated with results. How do you know which one to choose? You should definitely do plenty of research. You can compare companies at **www.money.co.uk**.

I personally trade with IG Index (**www.ig.co.uk**). They were the first major spread betting broker and are still one of the biggest. You might prefer to go with a company offering a particularly good introductory deal, but I would steer clear of very small companies as they may turn out to be unreliable.

Whoever you decide to go with, you must be comfortable with your account and broker. Don't accept anything less than first class service. Remind them that there are plenty of other brokers for you to choose from. If you have any questions, you can call them. Remember, they need your business – they spend a lot of money in staff wages to have helpful, professional, polite people at the end of the phone ready to get you going. If you don't get the service you're looking for, move on to the next firm.

When you sign up with a broker, you will have to fill out an online registration form and give some basic personal details. Spread betting brokers will usually want to ensure that you have a regular income and some savings. You don't have to be rich, but you have to show that you can afford to risk your money.

If you are a first timer, you should definitely look for a broker offering a demo account so you can practice before you start live trading. Some will allow you to have a demo account for several weeks. It's a useful way of getting familiar with the company's platform.

Most brokers now offer a smartphone app. I find this very useful. It allows me to manage my trades when I'm away from the office. I use the settings on the app to trigger various alarms to alert me when I hit profit targets. However, the smartphone app can be a dangerous tool if you struggle with patience and are prone to overtrading, a concept I will discuss further later.

4. A pot of money

You must set your own starting balance according to what you can afford to lose. If you are just starting out, keep it small. Don't put everything you have into the pot until you know what you are doing. While you are learning you will probably have to accept some losses, you may even blow out your first account, so you want to have some money left in the bank to start over with once you've learnt the ropes. Conversely, you need to have enough so that when you do have winning trades, the profits are enough to inspire you to keep going.

I suggest putting between £500 and £2000 into your first trading account. As I explained, it should only be about half of the total amount you have set aside to trade with. You can always top it up later.

Remember, trading should be for life; it's not a quick in-and-out gamble, so budget accordingly. Don't blow everything you have in six months and then have nothing left to trade with just as you're getting the hang of it. I've seen that happen all too often.

Also, don't forget you will have some overheads. Hopefully you will choose to invest a little money in some training, and you should budget a certain amount a month for a professional chart package. Trading is a business, your business, so you should invest in it.

You must protect your trading account because you cannot trade without money in your account.

5. A chart package

A chart package provides you with the technical analysis tools upon which you will base your trading decisions, so it makes sense to have the best you can afford. The more expensive the chart package, the more detail you will get and the more reliable the charts will be. You can get packages for free, but I wouldn't recommend basing important trading decisions on them.

I also recommend getting your charts from a different company than your broker. While the charts offered by spread betting brokers are improving all the time, you should be getting them from a company that specialises in them, not from a company that needs to provide them as part of its service. By keeping your spread betting broker and your chart package provider separate, you also avoid any conflict of interest issues.

Most companies will ask you to sign up for a monthly subscription. Decent chart packages start from around £18 a month. You can always upgrade your package when you start making more money. The top packages can cost hundreds of pounds per month, but it wouldn't be cost-effective to spend that kind of money until you are experienced and making a considerable profit from trading.

I personally like the following chart packages:

- **ShareScope (www.sharescope.co.uk)**
- **TradeStation (www.tradestation.com)**
- **ESignal (www.esignal.com)**
- **Telechart (www.telechart.com)**
- **AIQ Systems (www.aiqsystems.com)**

Of these, ShareScope is a UK company and the rest are American. I mainly use ShareScope and TradeStation, but I also have an account with AIQ.

6. Your time

The most frustrating thing I have seen people do is set up trades and then neglect them because they haven't scheduled the time to check on them. You can easily and needlessly lose money this way.

The advantage of online trading is that you can set your own schedule according to what fits best with your work and daily routine, but then you need to *stick to it*.

Your schedule may reflect the markets you choose to invest in. We have the opportunity to trade somewhere in the world 24-hours a day, almost seven days a week. When New York closes at 4pm local time, Japan and Australia are just opening. As they close, Europe is opening, and when Europe closes, New York is already open for business again. The only time the markets are all closed is between the time New York closes on Friday night (9pm GMT) and the time the Japanese and Australian markets open on Monday morning (sometime on Sunday evening GMT, depending on the season).

Once you're experienced, you can take the weekend off. While you are learning, I recommend using some time over the weekend to set up your trades for the following week. You can also use this time to study your charts, fine-tune your strategy and brush up your risk management plan.

7. Discipline

It sounds obvious that you need to be disciplined when you are trading, but it is easy to get tempted into decisions that are not part of your trading plan. There is plenty of temptation around when you are trading online, and a lack of discipline is the fastest way to lose everything. Without discipline, your other tools are all but useless. You must have the discipline to make a strong trading plan and stick to it.

You can have all the knowledge in the world, but if you don't have the discipline to put it into practice, you are not going to get very far. It's all very well knowing that you should put a certain trade on at a certain time, or that you should have a certain stop loss or profit target in place, but you have to actually press the button to set that stop loss or put that trade on. No one else is going to do it for you!

As I've already said, losing some trades is an inevitable part of your trading plan. You have to get your head around that and not feel disheartened when you lose money. The sooner you can master your emotions when you lose, or win, the sooner you will start trading well.

It's not just online information and flashing signals that can tempt you away from your plan. There's constant chatter about the economy and industry. Whether you're listening to the news, at a dinner party, or overhearing a conversation on the train, you hear people talk. You have to ignore virtually everything you hear, because these are the distracting opinions of others. You need discipline to ignore most of what you're hearing around you.

Imagine your friend phones you with a "hot tip" and you act upon it and you end up losing money. You're going to feel awful and your friend is going to feel worse. If your trading plan says that you don't listen to tips from friends, that you only trade according to what the signals within your indicator system tell you to do, then you can't feel bad about not listening to your friend's tip. Whether or not the tip comes good and makes money, you followed your strategy; it was your plan's fault you didn't act upon it. Next time it will be thanks to your plan that you do make money. Trust me, you'll feel better once that happens.

In all the years I spent playing football and all the years I've spent trading, I never had a greater test of my discipline than when I chose to run the London Marathon. So many times, I just didn't want to go on my training runs. Sometimes I had to force myself to put my kit on, which ended up being half the battle. During the Marathon itself I wanted to give up, so many times, but I forced myself to keep going. I just didn't let up on my discipline, despite every bone in my body screaming at me to stop. And I completed it.

You need to show similar, unswerving discipline in your trading.

COMPLETING THE LONDON MARATHON

8. Patience

In trading, timing is everything. If you don't make the right move at the right time, you can easily lose out on potential profit. But more often than not, it is about *not* making a move until you get the signal to do so.

Think of a lion, waiting for its prey. It will wait for hours if necessary, until it sees the right moment, until it knows it has the best chance of catching the prey and making the kill. It could be famished, but it knows if it acts rashly and pounces before the right moment comes, it will lose its chance of a meal. You need to behave this way and show this patience in your trading.

If it helps you to wait for the right moment sit on your hands. Seriously. I tell people this all the time. Learn to sit on your hands. As important as it is to *watch* your trades and take action when you get the relevant signal, it's important *not to do anything* before the time is right. It can be incredibly frustrating but you will learn the hard way if you don't control your impatience.

9. An open mind and willingness to learn

I believe we always have more to learn and absorb, no matter how expert we become in a field.

If you've traded before but you've become frustrated with your strategies, you need to wipe the slate clean and come at it from a different angle. If you are a complete newcomer then make sure you've done that exercise in the last chapter, freeing yourself up from negative emotions associated with financial decisions.

If necessary do it again, and keep doing it until you feel you are able to make decisions with as little emotion as possible. I won't say "no emotion" because I don't think that's possible. We all have emotions. The markets themselves are ultimately driven by human emotions, as investors get fearful or over-confident, but you have to suppress your feelings as much as you can.

Get educated and stay educated. Be wary of flashy talkers with fancy PowerPoint presentations who have never actually traded themselves. Learn from other traders and share information. Remember, you are not in competition with other traders; you are only actually in competition with your broker. Only your broker loses when you win. Other traders can make as much as you without it impacting your gains, and vice versa.

10. Your trading plan

The whole of the next chapter is dedicated to the making and implementation of your plan. A trading plan is a vital tool. You can't even begin before you've made a plan and without one you will likely lose money fast. You must write your plan down, either on your computer or iPad, or by hand on a piece of paper – it must be something you can put in front of you and keep referring back to.

You can know all the theory and you can practice as long as you like on a dummy account, but until you are trading with real money in real time, you won't understand how hard it is to stay disciplined and patient and make the right decisions. This is when a plan is necessary to keep your trading in order.

Another problem area is the fine line between neglecting your trades and overtrading. I've seen just as many people lose money through doing too little as doing too much.

Are you good with plants? Do you forget to water them and let them die? Or do you overwater them and kill them that way? It amazes me when I see people neglect plants. They are sitting right in front of you and you don't think to water them? If you are one of these people, think very carefully before you start trading. Maybe don't start trading until you've successfully kept a couple of plants alive! Managing your trades is a lot like caring for plants. Neglect them and you will lose out on banking the profit targets you hit. Overtrade and you might stop your trades from achieving their greatest potential.

It's like the game, *The Weakest Link*; making the decision when to bank the money is nerve wracking. Some people bank far too early and never reach the team's full potential. Some people risk a large pot of money by not saying "bank" when it's their turn, then they get a question wrong and lose the lot. Luckily, when you're trading, it's only you in charge of saying "bank", but the analogy still applies. Do it too early and you'll miss out on profit. Do it too late and you could lose everything. A trading plan will help you get the balance right.

CHAPTER ELEVEN:
YOUR TRADING PLAN

What goes in a trading plan

YOUR TRADING PLAN is your personal manual. It is basically the set of rules by which you will trade. You must make a good plan and stick to it. If it's not working, adjust it, but don't adjust it until you've given it long enough for you to get some meaningful results. A trading plan includes:

- Setting your budget
- Choosing your chart package
- Selecting the markets/vehicles you will trade
- Deciding how much you will risk on each trade
- Setting your profit targets and stop losses

Setting your budget and choosing a chart package were covered in Chapter 10. I will go on to look at the other points below.

Choosing your market and trading vehicles

Chapter Thirteen describes in more detail how spread betting works and why this is my preferred trading vehicle/method.

You also need to choose which markets you want to trade in. I often start by teaching beginners the forex (foreign exchange) market because most people have exchanged currencies before and can identify with doing it.

Deciding on your trading values

How much are you going to put on to each trade? My hard and fast rule is that I only risk 3% of my trading account on each trade, and I only expose 20% of my account at any one time. So, if I have £1000 in my account, I can trade with £200 at one time. If I'm not risking more than £30 (3% of my account) on each trade, I could place five trades that risk £30 each and two trades that risk £20 each to be trading with £190 in total at that time.

Setting your profit targets

I want to weep when I hear of people who have hugely successful winning trades but forget to bank any of it before the price goes down again. It seems so illogical, but people do it, all the time. Remember, you can look at one of your trades and think you are £400 up, but until you bank some of that profit, *it's not yours!*

There's a famous story of a trader who was £4m up and lost the lot because the trade did a nosedive before he banked any of it. It sounds absurd, impossible even, but it happened. You must bank your profits on a regular basis. Your profit targets must be written down, in black and white, as part of your trading plan.

Setting your stop losses

On every single advertisement you ever see for spread betting brokers, on every home page on every broker's website, you will read the disclaimer warning that spread betting can result in losses that are more than your initial stake. Those losses will come out of your trading account.

If you don't protect your trading account by setting stop losses, you could be wiped out with one losing trade. A stop loss is an order you place with your broker to automatically close a given trading position at a predefined price. Therefore, it stops losses from being magnified beyond a level you are comfortable with.

The advantage of having a good trading plan is that once you've written it you can follow it like a trained monkey. There's no thinking required. In fact you are better off *not* thinking. If you're constantly thinking about your plan, you will start tinkering with it unnecessarily. If you need a distraction, read a good book; save any clever thinking for your book club.

Remember, this type of trading is based on technical analysis. We're following patterns not opinions. This is why I sometimes feel people with a higher level of education are actually at a disadvantage, because they are prone to over-thinking things and can easily start second-guessing themselves and deviating away from the plan.

From what I've observed, most people are better traders when they are completely new to it than they are a year down the line. After 12 months or so you've got the emotional baggage from your experiences weighing you down and affecting you, making you think things over too much. You must try to suppress those feelings.

I'm like this when it comes to golf. I love golf, but I'm a fair-weather golfer. I love playing in the summer months, but you won't find me battling the bitterly cold winds and torrential rain that some obsessed golfers will face.

Every summer, the first time I go out, I play a fantastic round. I then get steadily worse until I hit a plateau and start to improve again. This is because in that first round, I have no expectations, I'm going out cold. I can't remember any of my bad rounds and bad shots from the year before. Everything feels fresh and easy; I'm not hampered by my past mistakes.

After a few rounds I start to think about the finer details of my swing and then it all starts unravelling. I start overcomplicating my swing. I'm hyper-aware of the angle of my shoulder and the position of my hips, my mind starts playing tricks on me, telling me I'm getting it all wrong, and suddenly I'm all over the place. Mentally, I'm closer to being a good golfer on the first day of the season than I am six rounds later.

Every six months, try to wipe that slate clean in your brain and pretend you are starting from scratch as a new trader!

Why you need a trading plan

There are four main reasons why you need a trading plan:

1. To prevent overtrading

When you first learn to trade, you will feel like you have a new toy to play with. Do you remember what you were like when you got your first PlayStation or iPhone? When you first got it, you probably wanted to play with it all the time. With video games and phones that's not necessarily a bad thing. But with trading, it's not a good thing. You can easily start to overtrade, over-expose your account, and stop your trades from achieving their maximum potential profit. A good plan will keep you on track and stop you from overtrading, as long as you stick to it.

2. To make controlled decisions

Your plan should stop you from making rash decisions based on random outside information that does not fit with your strategy. Following the rules of your plan, you will base your decisions on a pre-decided set of factors and will not be swayed by other outside influences, such as trading tips you hear from friends, or what you might read in the press.

3. To control your emotions

Your emotions are just waiting to trip you up, tempting you to buy when you shouldn't. As long as you've made a good plan, you've got an excuse not to go there, you have something to hide behind. Your plan should protect you from being tempted into impulsive moves. Furthermore, when things go wrong, you will feel so much better being able to blame your plan, rather than blame yourself, or your friend with the hot tip.

4. To avoid common pitfalls

Without a plan, you will fall into all the common traps that trip up traders and make them lose money fast, for example overtrading, impulse trading and not having a clear risk-management plan.

Theory versus practice

Is it all sounding too simple? Well it is, it's very straightforward. What's not straightforward is you.

I can't tell you how many people I've taught who get the theory of a trading plan perfectly but can't put it into practice. They become fantastic traders in the training sessions, using demo accounts, but then they go off and try to do it for real and end up coming back to me six months later having lost all their money.

They're usually quite humble about it, admitting that they didn't stick to the plan, that they made some impulse trades that didn't work out, or that they got bored and frustrated and took risks to make it all more exciting. I tell them not to beat themselves up (as we know, that will only make things worse), because their experience is all part of their education.

There's a huge shift when you start trading with your own money after doing it with virtual money on a dummy account; it becomes much harder to make the right decisions and stick to the plan. Imagine the difference between spending a week learning to land a plane in a flight simulator and then doing it for real. Handling the weight of the plane shouldn't be a problem, if you've already done it successfully in a simulator, but having the lives of 400 or so people in your hands would be a huge shift in pressure and responsibility; which is why pilots undertake such intense psychological training.

What most unsuccessful traders do

Whenever someone comes to me because they've lost a lot of money trading, before they even start telling me their story, I would be willing to bet big money on the fact that they didn't write a good plan or didn't stick to it.

The following is a list of the main reasons people fail at trading; most could be addressed by having, and sticking to, a good trading plan:

- **Overtrading**. By placing too many trades, or coming out of them too soon, you run the risk of not making as much profit as you could, or missing opportunities because your funds are mismanaged and you don't have enough left to put on an important trade that does fit your plan.

- **Risking too much**. By putting too much into a particular trade or over-exposing your trading account, you risk too much of your trading money and, again, could leave yourself without funds to trade with.

- **Failing to set stop losses**. When you don't set stop losses, you leave your account completely exposed. By doing this you risk losing everything. This is the main thing that brokers have to warn against in their disclaimer statements.

- **Setting stop losses that are too tight**. You can just as easily set your stop losses too close to your entry points, thereby not giving your trades enough time to run. Trades are like good wine, they need time to breathe; you don't open a good bottle of wine and drink it straightaway, you give it time to breathe.

- **Failing to set profit targets**. As I've mentioned before, if you don't set down in your plan what your profit targets are and then bank profits when you hit the targets, you could easily lose money that was once as good as yours. Nothing is more painful than the realisation you've done this. I can't even imagine the emotional rollercoaster of the guy I mentioned earlier who lost £4m!

- **Impulse trades**. Whether these are motivated by peer pressure, media hype, or a tip off from a friend who works in the city, they rarely work out in your favour. Even if they do, they give you a false sense of achievement because they weren't dictated by your plan and this will convince you'll get the same good result next time you deviate from your plan. The chances are, you won't.

■ **Boredom trades.** One of the worst things I see people do is to overtrade when they are bored. If you feel like putting a trade on because you're bored, yet it's not part of your plan, don't do it! If you get bored and there's nothing to do, walk away from the computer, get out of the house and switch your phone off, do the ironing, weed the garden. Do anything other than sit in front of your computer with idle, twitching hands.

Conversely...

What most successful traders do

Almost without exception, anyone I meet who makes a good income trading the money markets through spread betting as a swing trader has a good trading plan. Typically, they will be:

■ **Undertrading.** They will only have a modest amount of live trades placed at any one time.

■ **Setting profit targets and banking profit.** They will be protecting their trading account, fiercely, to ensure they don't lose out on profits.

■ **Setting stop losses at the right places.** They will ensure that their stop losses are in the right place, so that they are not too tight, which would mean missing out on profit, or too loose, running the risk of losing the whole stake.

■ **Disciplined.** This means resisting impulse trades or boredom trades and keeping to a schedule to ensure they manage their trades on a regular basis.

■ **Unaffected by losing trades.** No one can get it right every time. There isn't a trader in the world who knows exactly what the markets are going to do. No one can control or predict the actions of millions of people. Nothing is a safe bet and the markets really do humble you when you get it wrong. The smart trader isn't affected by losing trades. The smart trader just continues to trade according to their plan. You can't be ego-driven. It can't be about being right, or winning at all costs, or you will come unstuck.

Mastering your plan, mastering yourself

You can never fully master the markets. However, you can master yourself. By following your plan you can strengthen your discipline and work on your patience. You can amass knowledge and build up your mental resolve so that you can take the rough with the smooth and become a successful trader. You can do this – I did, so anyone can.

If you find that your trading plan works 60% of the time, then stick with it. Ignore the losses. If 40% of your trades are losing trades, you are still likely to end up in profit. Conversely, if your strategy is only working 40% of the time then you need to make some adjustments. Whatever you do, don't change your plan just because you're bored of it.

Remember, it's not a sprint, it's a marathon. As with marathon training, if you stick to the plan, you'll reduce the number of mistakes you make and avoid some of the associated pain. Plus, you're most likely to get to the end of the race. It took me many years to get it right and I still have plenty of losing trades, but far less than I used to.

In the third section of this book I will be telling you some of my trading stories to show you how, by sticking to my plan, I made money while others may well have been losing theirs.

CHAPTER TWELVE:
FOLLOWING THE PLAN

THIS IS THE tough part. It is so important to understand why you must follow your trading plan to the letter, and how easily you can get tempted to stray from it, that it necessitates a whole chapter. As I've said, it's easy to get the theory – putting it into practice is where most people come unstuck. So I'm going to try to give you as many tips as possible to help keep you on track.

Your plan is your trading strategy and, as with any strategy, you will get the most out of it by following it religiously.

Your strategy gives you a number of instructions. It tells you:

- Which trades to get into and when to enter them.
- How many pounds per point to bet (you decide this based on your account size).
- How much to risk (where to set your stop loss).
- When to bank your profits (where you set profit targets).
- When to come out of a trade (again, your chart indicator will give you the signal).

When you get a chart package, you will be able to look at the price movements of various products. Most charts will come with a free set of indicators that can calculate the best trades to enter, and signal the best entry and exit points. These indicators will give you signals alerting you to when the time is right to get into a certain trade.

Remember, the signals will alert you when it's time to get into the trade; they will not *get into the trade for you*. You have to physically go into your trading account and put the trade on, taking care to set your stop loss first.

The most important thing you must do is trust your charts and the signals generated by your system. Why? The indicators in your system are triggered by sets of mathematical formulae that you have no requirement to understand in order to follow. But because of this, you also must not second-guess them. If you deviate from the plan, even a little, you are altering the sample size, you are changing the statistical formula. You must stick to your plan.

It's all to do with probabilities. You cannot win every trade. Statistically you have to lose some. The signals on your charts, and the trading plan you will implement, are designed to make you win the statistically probable most times.

If backtesting shows that previous signals from a certain indicator have generated lots of winning trades, then the odds of this particular indicator giving you a winning trade are fairly high. It still doesn't guarantee that it will be a winning trade and you will make money, it just means that there is a high probability of it being a winning trade. Maybe 70 of the last 100 trades this indicator signalled you to put on were winning trades, and 30 were losing trades, then the indicator is working at a rate of 70% probability of success. If, on a whim, you decide not to take a trade that has been signalled, you are affecting probability; you are changing your strategy.

Imagine you have a weighted coin. It is weighted to land on heads. You toss it 100 times. It is not going to land on heads EVERY time, but it is going to land on heads perhaps 70 to 80 times because it is weighted. If you keep calling out HEADS, you will win those 70 to 80 times. If you randomly call out TAILS, by fluke you might get lucky that one time, but you are NOT playing to the highest probability, and out of 100 tosses, if you randomly call out both heads and tails, you may only win 50 to 60 times.

When you do something different, when you *deviate* from the plan that has been designed to win *most* of the time, you lower your odds of winning.

Before Bradley Wiggins won his time trial gold medal at the 2012 Olympics, he'd had an earlier disappointment. When interviewed he was asked if he'd do anything differently next time. He said no, of course he wouldn't do anything different. He knew if he stuck to the plan, if he did everything the way he always did, he would win gold. He knew he was the fastest cyclist in the world. He knew if he stuck to his plan and followed everything he had learned in training, he would give himself the best chance of winning the gold. You don't succeed by changing your plan in response to a setback.

Following the same routine – following the same trading plan every day – will help you, mentally. Sportspeople often have small rituals that they do before they start a game or a race. It's not usually about superstition, as some people tend to think, it's actually about mental preparation. It's a way of preparing the brain and the body to do all the things they usually do, to follow the plan.

When I was playing football, I had a routine. I had to put my shirt on last. That was my thing. I did that before every game I played. If I had a bad game, I wouldn't suddenly change the plan. I would stick to what I always did, knowing that it usually worked.

In sport you have to train your body, physically. In spread betting, you just have to train your brain to follow the rules. It should be a lot easier than playing a game of football or cycling in a race. But people find it hard. Maybe it's more like diving.

You're Tom Daley, you're an Olympic diver. You've been training since you were in primary school and you're about to dive for your first medal. You climb up the stairs and walk out on to that high diving board. You stand on the edge. You know you can do it, you've practised this dive countless times; you know you're good. You know all this, but if you hesitate, if you do something differently, like change the position of your feet or arms, the dive's not going to go right and you'll miss out on that medal.

It's the same with trading. You can have the best charts and indicator system, you can have the best plan, that's been fine-tuned through years of practice, but every single time you have to go into your trading account and actually hit the button to put the trade on at the right time. If you do something differently, if you hesitate and wait until the following day, you'll miss the right moment and potentially miss out on the maximum profit. To get the best statistical odds, you must do the same thing, every time.

Spread betting with a plan is smart trading. Spread betting without a plan is simply gambling.

In case you hadn't noticed yet, successful spread betting is:

- 1% mathematics and 24% psychology.
- 1% decision-making and 24% discipline.
- 1% time management and 24% patience.
- 1% facts and 24% faith.

Or...

- 100% following your plan.

You also have to forget about results. If you are focused on results you will trip yourself up. You can't control results, only your own actions. Forget about results, they will be what they will be. Focus on following the plan.

When Alex Ferguson walked into a changing room before a game, he wouldn't have said, "Right, lads, we're going to win 2-0 today." He would walk in and talk strategy. He would talk about the plan, about the best way, taking account of the opposition's strengths and weaknesses, to get the ball down the pitch and into the net. He would talk about how best to keep the ball away from the opposition's forwards and about the process of scoring goals, not how many goals he wants. If a football team keeps to their strategy they have the best chance of winning, just as you do with spread betting.

Stick to a carefully planned process and the results will take care of themselves.

CHAPTER THIRTEEN:
SPREAD BETTING

My preferred investment vehicle

AN INVESTMENT VEHICLE is anything in which you can invest. Stocks and shares, commodities, bonds, options, futures and ETFs are examples of products that can be traded, i.e. bought and sold. These days, we don't actually need to invest directly in these products to make money on their price movement; there are various methods that give us the opportunity to make money without actually buying or selling anything.

Spread betting is a method of making money from any investment vehicle by effectively simplifying and mimicking the investment. Instead of actually investing money and waiting for the value to go up, we bet a certain amount on whether the value of a product, or an index, or a rate, will go up or down.

There are a couple of other trading methods that allow you to make money from market movements without actually owning a product.

You can trade a product using a CFD (contract for difference). This is almost like a more formal way of spread betting. As with spread betting, you are not buying the actual product and, like spread betting, you are using leverage (i.e. you are only putting up a small deposit, called the margin, for the total number of shares you are buying). The difference from spread betting is that instead of betting, you are making a contract with your broker, basically an agreement to pay the difference. You don't pay stamp duty since you never actually own the share or product you trade, but you do pay tax because it is viewed as a profit-making (thus income-generating) transaction.

At the other end of the scale (much closer to gambling than spread betting) is a method of trading called binaries. Here, you are literally betting on whether the price of something will go up or down. It's a black or white loss or gain, and is based on the position on a sliding scale where you place your bet. The scale goes from 1 to 100. If you think, for example, the price of gold is going to go up tomorrow and you put one pound on the scale at 30, if the price goes up you "win" the number of points above 30, i.e. £70. If the price goes down, you lose the number of points below your entry point, i.e. £30. It's a bit more black and white than spread betting because you need to be confident you know which way the market is going to move.

In this book, we are looking primarily at spread betting, where you are betting a certain amount of money per point or pip that a product moves up or down. Again, we're not buying anything, we are just betting on the movement of the price of something. Thus we can spread bet on almost anything, including the price of stocks and shares, commodities, bonds, indices, options and ETFs. You never own anything, so there is no capital gains tax, and it is not seen as income so it is not taxable. The government still classes it as betting. (NB: This is true at time of writing.)

Some people take a while to get their heads around spread betting, so let's take a moment to make sure it's clear.

Basics of spread betting

In the good old days, say I wanted to buy some shares in a company called Lee's Boots. I would phone up my bank's share dealing service and they would buy the shares on my behalf directly from Lee's Boots.

Say the shares in the company are worth £10 each and I want to buy 100 shares. I need to go into my bank and write out a cheque for £1000. I will be sent a certificate saying I own these shares. While I own the shares, I will receive any dividends that are paid out.

When I want to sell the shares, perhaps because they have gone up to £11 six months down the line, I have to go back down to the bank, hand over my share certificate and I will receive a check for £1100. A nice tidy profit of £100 in six months, plus any dividends I earned. Not bad.

But I needed that £1000 available in the first place to do this and I also had the whole amount tied up in one company. So, even though I made £100 in six months, my entire £1000 investment was riding on Lee's Boots! I needed a lot of money to make relatively little and I had no money to invest elsewhere.

These days I can buy the same amount of shares with a small percentage of money using leverage. I go to my broker and say, "I want to buy 100 shares in Lee's Boots. However, I don't want to give you £1000 right now because I'd like some of it available to invest elsewhere. Can you buy them for me, and I'll give you a deposit of £100 with a promise to owe you the rest? When they go up the 10% I'm expecting, we can sell them, then I'll give you the balance that I owe you and I'll get my £100 deposit back plus the £100 profit I've earned."

Your broker agrees, and that's how you make money with only a small amount staked at the outset. The money that your broker is lending you is called the leverage. The deposit you give your broker initially is called the margin.

Spread betting goes one step further. You don't even bother with the contract. It's all happening too fast. You just place a bet with your broker on whichever way you think the price will move, and you bet a certain amount on each point it moves by.

The word *spread* refers to the difference between the "bid" (selling) price and the "offer" (buying) price. These prices are unique to each broker. Say you want to bet on the movement of the NASDAQ and it is standing at 3300. Your broker may give you a bid price of 3297 and an offer price of 3303. Another broker's bid and offer prices may be 3298 and 3302. In this scenario, your broker has a six-point spread while the other broker has a four-point spread. The smaller the spread the better, because the price has to move fewer points before you start to earn a profit.

In spread betting, we bet with pounds per point. You can bet any amount per point, such as £1, £5 or even £10. (N.B. in the forex market a point it called a pip.)

Don't worry too much what the point is actually worth, just think of it as the lowest measurement of movement. So, for example:

- If the share price of RBS moves from £2.55 to £2.56, it's moved up 1 point.
- If the FTSE 100 moves from 4810 to 4809, it's moved down 1 point.
- If EURUSD moves from 1.1906 to 1.1907 it's moved up 1 point (or pip).
- If USDJPY moves from 110.05 to 110.04 it's moved down 1 point (or pip).

It doesn't matter where the decimal point is. You don't have to think in terms of real value, or how many shares each point is worth, just look at the lowest unit of measurement. Every digit that the price or the index moves is worth one point or one pip.

Let's stick with the NASDAQ as the example. The following applies to all instruments; it doesn't matter if it's a company's stock, a commodity price, a currency pair, or interest rates.

Say your signals on your chart tell you that the NASDAQ is going to start going up. The real value (the *mid-price* in trading terms) of the NASDAQ is currently 3259. Your broker is quoting a bid price of 3257 and an offer price of 3261. You think it's going to go up so you enter the trade at the offer price of 3261 and you are placing a bet of £3 per point. You set your stop loss at 10 points below the NASDAQ's real value, i.e. you set a stop loss at 3249. That means if it drops 10 points, you get stopped out of the trade having only lost £30.

But your signals were correct and the NASDAQ starts going up. For every point it goes up over 3261, you get £3. Say it goes up by 50 points to 3311. You just made a profit of £150.

You see how much profit you can make but also how little the instrument has to move in the wrong direction for you to lose money. This is how people lose money spread betting; this is why your stop loss will save you.

To sum up, in spread betting, we are betting a certain amount (say £1, £5, £10, etc.) on the number of points or pips the price of an instrument will move up or down. That instrument may follow the price of a company's stock, or a currency pair, or a stock market index, or interest rates... it can be anything. For the number of points or pips it moves in the direction we've bet on, we earn that multiple of the amount we bet.

A spread bet on Lee's Boots

So let's go back to the example of me buying 100 shares in Lee's Boots. In the original example, I bought the shares. I gave my broker £1000 for 100 shares valued at £10 per share. When I sold them, at £11.00 per share, I pocketed £100 profit. The shares went from £10.00 to £11.00. Thus they moved 100 points.

Say I had gone to my spread betting broker when the share price was £10.00 and they'd given me an offer price of £9.98 and I'd placed a bet at £10.00 per point that the share price would go up, with a stop loss set at £9.90 (i.e. 10 points away from the mid-price of £10.00).

If I'm unlucky and the price goes down, I'll be stopped out of the trade when it hits £9.90 and I'll lose £100. See how it has only moved 10 points before I've stopped myself out, because I don't want to risk more than £100 on this trade? However, if the price rises from £10.00 to £11.00, i.e. it goes up 100 points. How much do I make?

I make £1000 (100 points x £10). This is a lot better than the £100 I made when I bought the shares outright and I did it without laying down the initial £1000 for the shares and also without tying up that whole £1000 in one investment. Plus, I guaranteed the most I could lose was £100 by setting my stop loss.

Now you can see how spread betting carries much greater risk, but offers much bigger potential returns.

Tax and spread betting

Why do you think the government doesn't tax spread betting?

When people bet, they usually lose money. In spread betting, because the pay outs can be so large, many people dive in without knowing what they're doing. They risk a lot and lose a lot.

If the government taxed people's earnings from spread betting, they would also have to allow people to write off their losses. Generally, people are losing more often than winning, so the government stand to lose more than they gain if they start taxing income and expenditure made via spread betting.

Plus, because spread betting brokers earn real income from their business, the government does tax the brokers. Since the brokers (en masse) are making huge profits off all the people losing from spread betting without knowing what they're doing, the government have clearly got it the right way around.

Long positions and short positions

One of the benefits of spread betting is that you can make money regardless of whether markets go up or down.

When you invested in shares in the old days, obviously you wanted the price to keep going up. You knew the price would probably go through a few dips, but ultimately the idea was that it would keep climbing in the long term. If you buy something in this manner – assuming it will go up in price – this is called going *long*.

These days, we can *short* the market to make money in a case where price goes down.

Shorting is a strange concept. In real terms it is when you sell something you don't physically own at one price in order to buy it back at a lower price. It's like buying in the future to sell now for a profit.

The risk is that if the price goes up instead of down, you are out of pocket because you've committed to buying those shares, or whatever you are shorting, at some point in the future in order to be "selling" them today.

In a way, in spread betting, you don't even need to understand the concept because in spread betting we are concerned only with the price of something moving – we never physically own anything whether we buy or sell. To stay in keeping with regular trading, we use the same terminology of going *short* the markets when we believe the value is going to move downwards and going *long* when we believe the value is going to move upwards.

This is what I love about spread betting. It doesn't matter what the markets are doing – we can always make money. We are going to be fine during times of economic crisis. In fact, when practised safely and smartly, spread betting gives the individual the opportunity to do particularly well in gloomy economic times.

While governments are scrambling around bailing each other out of billions of debt, and big investment banks are being hit with fines for insider trading and manipulating interest rates, and hedge fund managers are being sacked for mismanaging the investments of billionaires, you can be quietly making a few quid on the internet. Doesn't that put a smile on your face?

CHAPTER FOURTEEN:
LEARNING TO DRIVE YOUR VEHICLE

ASSUMING YOU KNOW how to drive a car, try and think back to a time when you didn't know how to drive. There was that time when you first sat behind the wheel and, chances are, it was terrifying. You were in control of this big, powerful machine and you didn't have a clue what to do. It took hours and hours of tuition and practice to learn how to drive. Now, it's second nature, you probably don't even think about it as you're doing it. That's how good you need to get at spread betting before you can think about making a decent income from it.

These days, I mostly operate as a day trader. I get in and out of trades the same day and I trade the most volatile market of all, the crude oil market.

The price of crude oil fluctuates hugely, on an hourly basis. Spread betting on the price of crude oil is like driving a Ferrari. If you've never driven before, we're not going to put you straight into a brand new Ferrari or you'd probably crash it. You have to learn on a nice, modestly sized, second-hand car first. And we won't let you drive on your own until you really have the hang of it. As my mate who taught me to drive said, "If you're still thinking about when to change gears, you're not ready to take your test."

First we're going to literally *build* your car. We're going to write your first trading plan and then you're going to learn how to *drive* it.

Choosing what to trade

You can trade any market you like but I wouldn't recommend starting off in a highly volatile market like crude oil. There are other markets and products that have certain idiosyncrasies that make them a little tricky to understand to begin with too.

Foreign exchange market

For several reasons, I like to teach people to trade the forex market when they are starting out. I think it's the best market to start trading in because:

- Most people have had experience of exchanging currency, so it's relatable;
- While currency is a highly volatile market, it is not like trading stocks and shares that could effectively completely collapse, so it provides a certain investment stability while having the fluctuations that can make good profits if you get into the right trades; and
- It is open 24 hours a day, and from when Australia and Japan open on Sunday night (UK time) until the time New York closes on Friday night.

There are nine major currency pairs that I focus on trading:

1. AUDUSD (the Australian dollar against the US dollar)
2. EURCHF (the euro against the Swiss franc)
3. EURGBP (the euro against the British pound)
4. EURJPY (the euro against the Japanese yen)
5. EURUSD (the euro against the US dollar)
6. GBPUSD (the British pound against the US dollar)
7. USDCAD (the US dollar against the Canadian dollar)
8. USDCHF (the US dollar against the Swiss franc)
9. USDJPY (the US dollar against the Japanese yen)

If you think about it, you've probably already traded the forex market already, and perhaps successfully.

Say you were due to go on holiday to Australia; then you would need to buy some Australian dollars. You probably started keeping an eye on the exchange rate of the GBP against the AUD for a month or so before you left. When you saw it was on an uptrend, when you felt you would get the most AUD for your GBP, you probably went to the bank and changed your money. You would feel good knowing you got a few more Aussie dollars than if you'd exchanged your money the week before.

So trading currency pairs is not a new concept to you. Great. That's one part of your first plan in the bag for now.

Money management

It is entirely up to you how much you are going to put into your trading account. You will set your own budget and you can write your own money management rules. For now, I'm going to tell you the rules I trade by. I'm teaching you to drive in my car. It's a good little runner, my car.

Basically my rules are as follows:

- I only ever risk 3% of my account on each trade; and
- I only ever expose 20% of my account at any one time.

That's it! Couldn't be easier.

So now let's plug a few figures in to get a taste for how this is going to work.

Say I have decided to put £2000 into my trading account. That means I can risk up to £400 on live trades at any one point in time. I don't have to risk the whole £400. Maybe it's a slow period and at one moment I only have £300 at risk, but I never go over the £400. That's my maximum total risk.

Now, let's say I get a signal to take a long position on the GBPUSD when it is at 1.4901. The maximum I can risk on one trade is 3% of my account, that's £60.

Now I have another choice to make. Do I want to bet a greater number of pounds per point and make profits faster, but have a tighter stop loss, or do I want to bet fewer pounds per point and give myself more breathing room for the trade to go the wrong way before I get stopped out of it?

Either way, I risk the same amount. Let's look at three different scenarios to help you get the picture.

Betting £1 per point

I bet £1 per point. My maximum risk is £60. I don't want to lose more than £60, so I must set my stop loss at 60 points away from the entry point of 1.4901. If I'm unlucky and my signal was wrong, and GBPUSD falls by 60 pips to 1.4841, I will be stopped out of the trade and will have lost £60. (Imagine if it kept on falling and fell 200 points to 1.4701 – I would lose £200.)

As long as my signals are on track and the rate moves up, say to 1.5051, i.e. 150 points, I could bank a profit at that point of £150.

Now let's try that with £5 per point.

Betting £5 per point

I bet £5 per point. My maximum risk is £60, so I must set my stop loss at 12 points away from the entry point of 1.4901. If I'm unlucky and my signal was wrong, and GBPUSD falls by 12 pips to 1.4889, I will be stopped out of the trade and will have lost £60. (Now imagine if it kept on falling and fell 200 pips to 1.4701 – I would lose £1000.)

As long as my signals were correct and the rate moves up, say to 1.5051, i.e. 150 points, I could bank a profit at that moment in time of £750.

Now let's try with £10 per point.

Betting £10 per point

I bet £10 per point. My maximum risk is £60 so I must set my stop loss at only 6 points away from the entry point of 1.4901. If I'm unlucky and my signal was wrong, and GBPUSD falls by just 6 pips to 1.4895, I will be stopped out of the trade and will have lost £60. (Now imagine if it kept on falling and fell 200 points to 1.4701 – I would lose £2000.)

As long as my signals are on track and the rate moves up to 1.5051, i.e. 150 points, I could bank a profit at that moment in time of £1500.

Hopefully this example has shown you how vital it is to set your stop losses.

Obviously the more pounds per point you bet, the faster you can earn profit, but the quicker you could lose your £60 risk and be stopped out of the trade. You don't risk more than the 3%, the £60, on each trade, so the more pounds per points you bet, the closer to your entry point that stop loss gets.

I usually suggest that beginners start by betting £2 per point.

Example of two new traders

For a bit of fun, and to see this take shape in real terms, let's follow two people as they get to grips with trading for the first time. To give you an idea of who they are, let's look at how they did on their driving tests.

1. When Alice learnt to drive, she practised most days for three months before she took her test. On the day of her test, she found it easy to remember all the rules. She always remembered to check her mirrors and indicate, and she changed up and down the gears smoothly. She ended up back at the test centre with her licence.

2. Betsy took a crash course the week before her test. She went into her test confident she knew what she was doing, but she crunched the gears, jumped a set of traffic lights, and almost killed a little old lady on a pedestrian crossing. To top it all off, she ripped a wing mirror off the car as she took a bend too tight pulling into

the test centre car park. The instructor, who suffered whiplash from one of Betsy's unnecessary emergency stops, gave her a bill for the car damage and told her not to come back for another year.

Alice's story

Alice works in PR in central London and lives in Richmond. She lives alone and has a great social life. She gets home from work on weeknights at 7pm and, if she's not going out with friends, she tries to get to the gym by 8pm.

Alice has £5000 in her savings account and a steady job, so she has decided to try her hand at spread betting. She's been on a course and she's opened a dummy account, so she's practiced for a few weeks. She's decided that she will manage her trades every day for half an hour in the evening when she gets home from work. She'll also spend an hour on Saturday morning studying her charts and setting up trades for the following week.

Alice has bought a chart package with an indicator tool that will show her the daily momentum of her chosen market, the forex market. She has put £1000 into her trading account with her chosen spread betting broker.

On Monday, Alice opens her chart package and looks at her EURUSD chart. She sees a series of candlesticks. They show her the movement of the EURUSD rate over the past couple of months.

There are four points on every candlestick:

1. The very top of the upper thin vertical line shows the highest price for the day.
2. The top of the thick candle is the open or closing price (depending on which was the higher).
3. The bottom of the candle is the open or closing price (depending on which was the lower).
4. The bottom of the lower thin line is the lowest price for the day.

If the opening price was lower than the closing price (i.e. the price has gone up by the end of the day), the candlestick is usually green or white, but they can be any colour the user chooses.

If the opening price was higher than the closing price (i.e. the price has gone down by the end of the day), the candlestick is usually red or black, but again they can be any colour the user chooses.

In the following charts, black candles denote up days and grey candles denote down days.

Candlestick anatomy

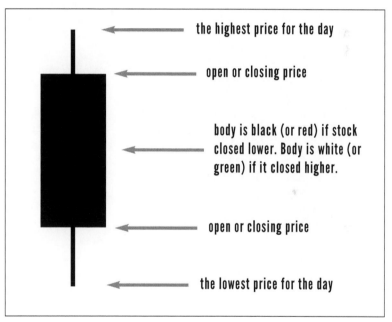

On opening the EURUSD chart, Alice sees that today's candlestick is grey (red). The candlesticks for the last week have been grey (red). Alice does nothing.

EURUSD chart showing a week of grey (red) candlesticks

The second chart Alice opens is her AUDUSD chart. On this one, the candlesticks have been grey (red) for five days.

AUDUSD chart showing five days of grey (red) candlesticks

Again, Alice does nothing.

It's the same frustrating story with the EURCHF and the EURGBP.

The next chart Alice opens is her EURJPY chart and she can see that today's candlestick is black (green), after a long series of grey (red) candlesticks. This is Alice's signal to get into the trade.

EURJPY chart showing today's candlestick to be black (green)

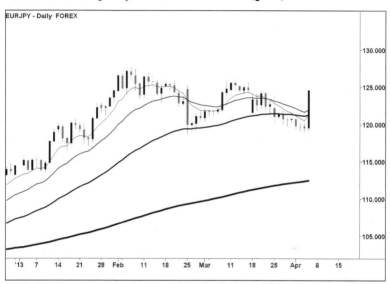

Alice opens her trading account in order to get into the trade in a long position. The first thing she decides upon is how much to risk on the trade. She has a pot of £1000 and her trading plan is to risk a maximum of 3% on each trade, so her maximum risk is £30. She can either bet £2 per point and set her stop loss at 15 pips away, or she can bet 20p per point and set her stop loss at 150 pips away.

Both would result in a maximum loss of £30, but because of the volatility of the forex market she decides to go with the second option in order to give the trade room to breathe.

The next two charts she opens are the GBPUSD and the USDCAD. Both of these charts also show black (green) candlesticks today, after a series of grey ones. Again, Alice goes to her trading account and enters the trades, again in long positions, at 20p per point, and with her stop loss set at 150 points away from her entry point.

So today, Alice has placed three trades. She has risked a total of £90 (3%, or £30 on each trade) and has thus exposed 9% of her trading account, which is well within the maximum 20% she can expose, leaving her room to enter more trades tomorrow if she gets the signals to do so. Alice closes her computer and goes for a run.

Don't you just hate her already?

Betsy's story

Betsy loves the champagne lifestyle and dreams of winning the lottery and going around the world on a yacht with Mr. Right. She's prone to a bit of gambling; she loves the thrill of it. She's even been to Las Vegas a couple of times. Every week Betsy buys a lottery ticket; she's sure the right numbers will come to her one day. She also buys around five scratch cards during the week. She's recently started going to bingo on a Thursday night.

Betsy is currently working as a waitress at a busy restaurant in the City. Her career plan includes marrying an investment banker (as insurance in case the lottery win never pans out). A couple of them have caught her eye but, moments later, so have their wedding rings. She's sure her Mr. Right is going to walk into the restaurant any day now.

Betsy has recently inherited £2000 from her grandmother who died just after Christmas. Her latest plan is to turn that money into £1m in under a year. Then she'd be able to get the flash car, join the fancy gym and holiday on Necker Island, which is where she hears all the real multi-billionaires hang out. She's overheard plenty of banking gossip as she's been serving Pinot Grigio and Dover sole. She's sure she's got all the tips she needs. It's a plan!

Betsy keeps hearing about this company called 'Crude Oil' – she hears the bankers talk about it as if it's the second coming. People seem to be making loads of money in this company, especially (she's pretty sure she's heard) something about its shares having great futures. Betsy reckons it must be the coolest, fastest growing company out there and she feels pretty pleased with herself, like she's been in the right place at the right time to have heard about it. She imagines buying so many shares that she attracts the attention of the company's CEO (who, in her imagination, is a 42 year-old recently divorced George Clooney look-a-like).

The day that Betsy's inheritance money comes into her account, she can't wait to get home and open a trading account and buy shares in "Crude Oil".

After a long Google search to find a broker, Betsy opens her trading account, transfers her £2000 into it and does a search for 'Crude Oil'. She's pretty shocked to find out that each 'share' costs £75, but at this point, she's so excited, she adopts a reckless in for a penny, in for a pound attitude.

With her £2000 Betsy buys what she assumes is 22 shares. She's shocked that her broker charges a hefty fee, so in the end she's only got enough for 20 shares. She goes to bed and can't wait to get up the next day and see how much she makes. She's got the day off so she can watch how the price goes up all day.

The next day Betsy gets up and logs on to her account, but alas! She is distraught to see that her 20 'shares' have plummeted in price and are now only worth £1000. She quickly sells them and although this leaves her with only £900 (after she pays the broker another fee), she's sure she's had a lucky escape. She must have misheard something and she resolves to concentrate harder on what the bankers are talking about when she serves them their crème brûlée the following day. She tries to ignore the fact that she just lost £1100 in less than 24 hours.

Before we start tearing our hair out, or phoning Betsy's mother, let's check back in with Alice.

Back to Alice's story

Alice has been checking her charts every day this week. It's Friday and nothing has changed. There have been no new signals. The charts that had black candlesticks still have black candlesticks, and the grey ones have grey ones. There's not been a lot to do and Alice has been a little frustrated.

On Wednesday, she did bank £100 of profit from her EURUSD trade, which climbed 50 points quickly. She's stayed in the trade because the candlestick on her chart is still black. She has also moved her stop loss up so that it is 15 points away from the point at which she banked her profit (making that point almost like a new entry point). This means that, whatever happens now, Alice cannot lose on this trade.

Alice would love to get into some new trades so that there's more going on, she's even had a good tip on a stock from a friend, but her trading plan at the moment is to trade only the forex market, and only base her trading decisions on her signals from her momentum-based indicator.

So Alice does nothing.

Back in Betsy world

Betsy is very, very excited. She was serving a couple of older bankers at lunch today. They weren't very attractive, so it was a no go on the husband quest, but she did overhear a very interesting conversation. She heard that they were going to buy shares in a company called Northern Rock because they were so cheap at the moment and the price was sure to shoot up any minute now. Betsy can't wait to get home and invest her remaining £900 in Northern Rock shares.

Of course we all know how that story ends. Poor Betsy.

Alice cracks it

After one month, Alice has managed to enter two more trades. She's in a short position on the GBPUSD and has banked £100 in profit from it so far. She also went long on the USDCAD but unfortunately she was stopped out of that trade for a loss of £30. She also got stopped out of her AUDUSD for a loss of £30. She's banked another £100 from the EURUSD trade and has moved her stop loss up again.

After her first month, Alice has banked £300 of profit and has lost £60. She's £240 up overall. Which is great as she just got a speeding fine and a parking ticket in the same week. So she *is* human after all!

CHAPTER FIFTEEN:
IS TRADING FOR YOU?

WHO ARE YOU? Are you a university graduate? Do you hold a PhD? Did you leave school at 16? Do you have no formal education? Are you male? Female? Young? Old? Retired? A parent? Married? Single?

Whatever your answers, they have absolutely no bearing at all on whether you will be a successful trader. The only thing that will determine whether you are a successful trader is your ability to learn some simple rules and follow them with rigid discipline.

Are you a Betsy or an Alice? Be honest with yourself. If you know you're a Betsy, trading is probably not for you at the moment. However, just because you're a Betsy today, it doesn't mean you can't become an Alice down the line. Test yourself with other projects, work on your discipline, practice learning new skills... and don't give your driving instructor whiplash next time you take your test.

So, you don't need a degree and you don't need huge amounts of cash – you just need basic tools and the right attitude.

Remember, timing may be a factor, too. If you've never traded before and you've read this book thinking, "I'd quite like to give this a go," but you know you don't have the time in your life right now to get the training, don't rush into it now. Do it when you have the time to invest in training and practice. If you rush in without understanding it and knowing what you're doing, you will probably lose money and never go back to it again.

You have to stay committed. Trading isn't something that you can pick up overnight. It takes a lot of time and practice. You need the time, as well, to get a good ratio of winning trades and to be able to see the results. Maybe after six months you're only winning 55% of your trades because you made some wrong turns when you started out. A year down the line that figure could be closer to 65% or 70% winning trades. You have to give it time.

Only you can set your budget and time frame, but don't give up after six months, give it at least a year if you can. You need to stick at it for a year to know if it's for you. Six months in you're still going through teething troubles; a few bad results could dampen your spirits, you could be going through a bad patch after a good start, you need to get over that hump and hopefully hit your stride again. I think you can only really judge how you're doing after a year.

When I see people give up after a few weeks, my heart sinks. They are often people who could get quite good with a little more practice, but they get frustrated and disheartened by losing a few trades, and they walk away angry and disappointed. They get caught up in a vicious cycle of making mistakes, leading to more frustration and a loss of patience and even *more* mistakes. You must stay patient, you must stay disciplined.

LACK OF PATIENCE AND DISCIPLINE = OVER TRADING = MISTAKES = STRESS = OVER TRADING = LOSING MONEY = OVER TRADING = STRESS

Protect your account

As I said at the beginning of this section, your trading account is your essential trading tool. Think less about how much money you are making, think more about protecting your capital because you literally can't trade without money in your account.

Any good spread betting broker will check that you have an income and savings before they allow you to open a trading account. Once it's open and once you have put your money in it, it is up to you to take care of it by setting a watertight risk strategy. This means setting a strict limit of how much money you will leave exposed at any one time, and remembering to set a stop loss on every trade.

Forgetting to set a stop loss is like leaving your wallet full of money on a park bench for several days. You could get lucky; you could come back and find it hasn't been touched. But you're leaving an open wallet on a park bench; you can't expect any cash to be left in it when you come back to get it.

You must protect your trading account like your wallet; you wouldn't leave your wallet exposed to pickpockets, and you wouldn't leave it lying around on a park bench, so don't leave your trading account over exposed by putting too many trades on at any one time. And set your stop losses!

"Oops, I forgot to set my stop loss," is as useful as saying, "Oops, I left my wallet full of cash on a park bench last night." You can but cross your fingers and hope. Not an effective way to run a business.

There's a scene in *Top Gun* when Maverick (Tom Cruise) is being reprimanded by his Lieutenant, Jester, for breaking off from his wingman and flying solo according to his own rules. His flying was admirable, but he endangered lives and in the end, the result of the exercise shows that, had it been a scenario in the real world, he would have been killed. "You never, *never* leave your wingman," Jester warns Maverick.

In trading, you are your money's wingman. You *must* stick by your money and watch it and make sure it doesn't fly off, solo, and do its own thing by its own rules. If you don't stick by it, it could easily get 'killed' by enemy fire!

I am trying to get you thinking like a pilot or a solider, or a naval officer. Military personnel are trained to follow the rules to the letter without questioning them. That is what you need to do in trading. Trust that your charts and indicator system are giving you the best instructions. Don't second-guess them and implement your own ideas. This is not a time to get creative; this is not a time for emotion.

There is no magic formula

If someone tells you they have the magic formula to being a successful trader, that they know how to make huge pots of money overnight, and they're willing to sell you this magic formula... then they are right. They do have a magic formula for making money... for themselves. They are going to make a fortune making you and a bunch of other suckers pay to listen to them talk about how you can make money if you have the discipline to stick to a plan. They are not selling you the discipline to do it.

There is literally no magic formula except for your own ability to stick to the plan and follow the rules, which are, in the simplest terms:

- Don't over-expose your account.
- Set your stop losses.
- Manage your position (i.e. choose when it is best to bank profits and when to let them run).

That's it!

If you do have the spare capital to invest in learning a new skill and to place some trades, if you do have the discipline to write and follow a trading plan, if you do have the time to set aside a few hours a week to manage some simple trades, then there should be nothing stopping you. You could be on your way to making a nice extra monthly income from spread betting.

Just fasten your seatbelt (put your risk management in place), put on your wingman's cap (don't over expose your account), get into your flight simulator (start your training), and away you go.

PART THREE

TRADING STORIES

IN THIS SECTION, I'm going to share some of my trading stories to give you real-life examples to back up the theory you've read up to this point. Your experiences may be similar or completely different to mine. The important thing is that, like me, you keep trying and learning. Hopefully you will learn from your mistakes and will incorporate your successful strategies into your trading plan, as I have.

Many of my trading decisions are based around trading wave patterns in the markets. If you've never traded before, think of it in terms of waves on a beach. My four-year old daughter and I love to play a game where we chase the waves in and out, while trying not to get our feet wet. When a wave comes in we run up the beach away from the sea; when the wave goes out we chase it back into the sea, bravely going as far as we can before it starts to come in again. Sometimes we get the timing wrong and the wave comes crashing in faster than expected and we get our feet wet. We have so much fun and we always end up falling about laughing.

When I look at a trading chart as I'm getting ready to trade, I base the majority of my trading decisions on the wave patterns that I see. Price waves go up and down just as the waves on the beach come in and out. If you choose the right wave, you can make money without getting your feet wet. This is the basis of my trading.

After many years of trading the markets, I have made my own interpretation of these wave patterns and I enter and exit trades based on my own set of rules. I know that if I follow these rules I am likely to make money; if I don't, I run the risk of losing money. There are many different ways to make money from the markets, my wave strategy is just one of them.

The examples of my past trades I describe below are short-term trades. I use short-term trades to bring in an income, but the strategies I describe can also be used for longer-term investment purposes.

You can make money to the downside of a trend as well as to the upside, and by combining wave patterns you could pick some very profitable market tops and bottoms. I may think an FX pair, stock or commodity looks cheap (undervalued), but if I don't get my wave pattern signal, I won't buy it. If I look to trade a market that I perceive to be undervalued but I have no entry signal, I'm just trading randomly.

Don't be naive and assume that when a price has lost significant value that it is automatically a good buying opportunity. It isn't until you get a technical signal that it is safe to dip your toe in the water and get into the trade.

I use around six different strategies in my trading. The two I use most often are my Pro Trading-System (PTS), and my Dynamic Divergence strategy.

My Pro-Trading System (PTS)

Many traders struggle when they get started and it was no different for me. Learning to trade is a real test of patience and discipline. There is so much information out there – so many different factors influencing your choices – that it is easy to get confused, lose confidence and become disillusioned about trading. Our brains can only process a few pieces of information at one time, so if we are bombarded by too many possibilities it can become overwhelming. This is why we need to stick to a clear and concise, easy-to-follow trading strategy. If you do not have a way to pick up clear buy and sell signals then you are not following a trading strategy.

I had been trading for several years – using many different types of computer systems and charts – when I felt inspired to design a bespoke, integrated trading system that would make my life easier. I really felt like there was a gap in the market for a very powerful, fine-tuned, user-friendly system. I used all my previous experience and knowledge to incorporate the best indicators, algorithms and trading strategies. I then worked with an expert writer of computer code for trading systems to build it into a computer package.

The result was the Pro-Trading System (PTS). It is a clear, easy-to-use system that quickly and automatically processes a huge amount of information. It is based on a number of algorithms – an algorithm being a step-by-step procedure for making a calculation.

There are two types of strategy built into the PTS: a *momentum strategy* and a *reversion to the mean strategy*. I want to identify when a market is going to start a new trend but I also want to get a signal when the price has dropped to an area where I think it is cheap enough to buy. I'm a very visual person so I designed all my signals on the PTS to be colour-based.

In the charts generated by my PTS, when I see a green candlestick after a series of red ones, it is telling me that buyers now have control and it's time to enter a new long trade. Conversely, when I see a red candlestick appear after a series of green ones, it tells me that the buyers are running out of steam and now the sellers are taking control, so I get into a short trade. It's when there is the change, from green candles to red candles or red candles to green candles, that I have my signal to enter a trade. In more advanced trading, I can also short on red and cover my trades when the candles turn green. The PTS does all the work in identifying trades to take and entry points; all I have to do is enter the trade with my broker. I have also fitted it with email alerts and audio alerts so I can walk away from my screens and still receive the signals.

The PTS automatically scans the markets every day in order to give me my next signal and everything is processed and calculated automatically. This means a new user doesn't need to understand the calculations behind the system, they just need to be able follow its signals. It is a bit like a finely-tuned car. You don't need to know what goes on under the bonnet, you just need to know when to hit the accelerator and the brake and it will get you from A to B in the most efficient way.

When I introduce the PTS to new traders they tend to love it because it is so simple. It tells them the optimal entry prices and profit targets, and it scans the markets, producing new buy and sell signals, and new short signals, in a matter of seconds. It also indicates when the markets could go into sideways trading patterns. It ultimately takes a lot of the uncertainty out of trading and gives new traders something structured to follow. The ones who follow it often get good results and steady profits.

Since 2008, when we got the PTS up and running, I haven't looked back. I do sometimes use other systems for certain trades, especially when I am day trading, but the majority of my trades are made using the PTS. It makes my life easier. I live such a busy life, mentoring and running a live trading room. The PTS means that I can simply turn on my PC and check to see whether I have any alerts to do anything. It's a lot quicker than going through hundreds of charts every time!

In the following trade examples I'm going to show you some of the most profitable trades I have taken using the PTS. As the charts in this book are in black and white, the green long trade signals are the darker candlesticks, and the red sell or short candlesticks are a lighter colour.

Please note that this is a different colour scheme to that used on charts elsewhere in this book that do not have the PTS overlaid on them. At all times I have stated the colour on the original chart and also the colour as it appears in the book to make this clear.

First of all, the following two charts show an example of the difference between a normal chart and a chart with the PTS on. You can see that on Chart 1 (without the PTS) there are lots of light (green) and dark (red) candlesticks. The price swings around a lot and this can play with the emotions of a novice trader.

Chart 2 is the same chart but with the PTS overlaid on to it. See how the candlesticks stay dark (green) all the way up in the trend. By keeping you in the trend, it allows you to make more money.

Chart 1: Normal price chart

Chart 2: Price chart with the PTS overlaid

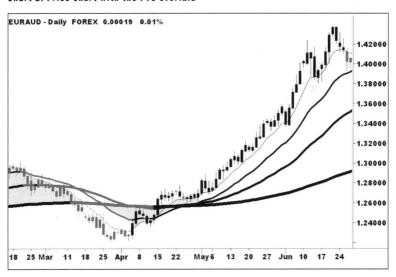

Dynamic Divergence Using the MACD

Another trading strategy I use, in fact one of my favourite strategies, is my Dynamic Divergence strategy using the MACD indicator. Later in this section, I'm going to demonstrate how I caught some tops and bottoms of the markets by adding a very simple MACD (Moving Average Convergence Divergence) indicator to price charts. This is displayed at the bottom of the chart, underneath the record of the price action.

The MACD is a trend-following momentum indicator that shows the relationship between two moving averages of prices. It signals when market momentum is increasing or decreasing, which is monitored alongside price movement to show where there is a divergence (i.e. the two lines start moving in opposite directions, price dropping as momentum increases, or price increasing as momentum slows).

The MACD is calculated by subtracting the 26-day exponential moving average (EMA) from the 12-day EMA. A 9-day EMA of the MACD, called the *signal line*, is then plotted on top of the MACD, functioning as a trigger for buy and sell signals.

What I am looking for is a market that has gone up too much, or dropped too low and is due a reversal – to indicate this I'm looking for a wave pattern called a *divergence*, as shown by the MACD. There are two types of divergences: *bullish* and *bearish*.

Thinking of this in terms of what buyers and sellers are doing, the price only falls so far before buyers begin to think it is undervalued. However, it can be very difficult to time when to enter the trade. The MACD shows when the trend to the downside is losing its strength and there could be a good opportunity to buy an undervalued market. The importance of using this indicator is that we don't want to be buying something that is falling with strong momentum and will keep on falling.

We have seen some stocks go to zero (think of some of the banks during the last financial crisis) and this could happen again. So when the price is falling hard we look for the MACD indicator line to start rising. This indicates that a divergence is setting up. The price is losing strength to the downside but we are also seeing buyers come into the market at these low levels, indicated by the MACD indicator line moving upwards.

This is called a *bullish divergence* as price and momentum are diverging as buyers come in to the market. When this starts to happen, it's my signal to get into the trade in a long position. The reverse would be the price rising while the MACD line starts moving down (a *bearish divergence*), which is a signal to close out a long trade or, for more advanced traders, get into a short trade.

I describe this wave pattern as being like running a marathon without any fuel left in the tank. At some point, you are going to stop or fall over because you don't have any carbohydrates left in your body to keep going. Think of the MACD indicator as the fuel gauge in the market – at some point, it will show that the market is out of fuel and is due to reverse.

The following charts illustrate bullish and bearish divergence.

Bullish divergence, Dow Jones Futures

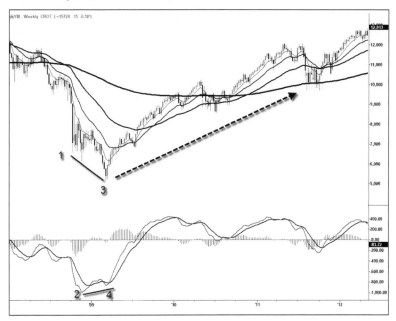

After a collapse in the stock markets due to the recession from 2007 to 2009, there was a major bullish divergence at the start of 2009. This happened to be the low in the stock market for the last five years. The chart shows that the price fell very hard, all the way down to 7000 in the Dow Futures market (1), and this was confirmed with the MACD lines (2).

However, this was not the end of the selling pressure as the price soon dropped another 1000 points down to 6000 (3). This last drop in price was not confirmed by the MACD lines (4), as they were not lower than the previous low (2). Price was soon due a rally higher because the short sellers had started to run out and now new buyers had started to enter the markets. There was now had a major bullish divergence in place and the price never looked back – it doubled in three years.

Bearish divergence, crude oil

The crude oil chart above is a clear example of a bearish divergence signal. The initial trend is up as the price of crude goes from $96 to $110 (1). The MACD indicator lines below the chart (2) have peaked and we then see the price fall back from $110 to around $104 over the summer months.

Following the price of oil, moving in a range of $2 to $4, we see the price breakout to a new high, to £112 (4). But take a look at the MACD lines now. The price has reached $112 but they are not at the same level as the previous peak when the price was near $110 (4). This shows that crude oil's price will not stay at the current high levels and we will see a price drop coming soon. We are basically running out of buyers on the trend to the upside and this is confirmed with the lower MACD lines. This is evident when price falls from £112 to almost $92 in the next three months.

CHAPTER SIXTEEN:

CRUDE OIL

What trading crude is about

CRUDE OIL IS one of several commodities that are traded on the global markets and is the most volatile market of them all. With such wild price fluctuations, on a daily basis as well as in the long term, there's the potential to make a lot of money from trading the crude oil market. Of course this also makes it the riskiest market to trade. It is known in the financial world as 'the widower market' because it can literally destroy people. So I always advise beginners to steer well clear of crude oil.

Why is crude oil such a volatile market? Well, the world literally depends on crude oil to survive. We need it to drive our cars and fly our aeroplanes. We use its by-products to make a vast list of everyday consumable items, from concrete to newspaper ink, from insulation material to camera film, from candles to tyres, and from contact lenses to golf balls. The world consumes an estimated 88m barrels of crude oil *every single day*.

Crude oil – also known as petroleum – is obtained from drilling into the earth and extracting the raw product from naturally occurring oil reserves. We know that these reserves are not going to last forever and our seemingly insatiable appetite for crude oil is fast becoming a real global concern, with some estimates suggesting we may only have 40 years left before we run out. Alternative sources of power are being sought but we are a long, long way off finding a major renewable replacement for fossil fuels. While our dependency on petroleum remains so high, crude oil will remain a hotly traded market.

It's our total dependence on this finite source of power and the fact that only a handful of countries own the world's major oil reserves that contribute to making the crude oil market so volatile. In addition, every Wednesday at 3.30pm GMT, the US Energy Information Administration (EIA, the US Department of Energy's statistical and analytical agency) publishes a report on the oil market that can send the price on quite a rollercoaster ride.

The daily fluctuation in the price of a barrel of oil is directly linked to supply and demand. When more oil is produced than is needed, the price will drop; when demand is higher than supply, the price will go up. It is also greatly affected by world events, especially wars, and when there is political unrest in the Middle Eastern oil-producing countries. Any hint of an oil shortage sends the price soaring, but it can just as easily fall sharply when demand is met.

The chart below shows the fluctuations of crude oil from 2003 to 2008.

Crude oil

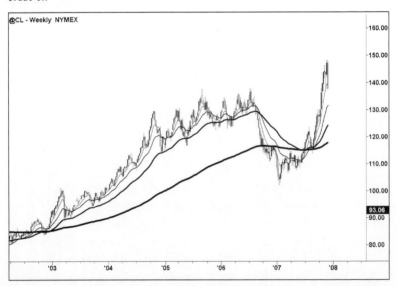

Watching crude oil rise to $150 a barrel

I had been trading as a hobby for 14 years, and as a professional for about four years, before I went anywhere near the crude oil market. To be honest, I wasn't even really aware of it for many years. When I started trading I had primarily focused on stocks and shares, and then I became interested in the forex market. It wasn't until 2006 that I began hearing people talk about crude oil and I got interested. There was a bull run (meaning prices were rising and were expected to carry on going up), so I decided to venture into it.

Over the years I have learnt that trading with the trend is far easier than counter-trend trading. Even though I have strategies for counter-trend trading, it is far less stressful going with a trend then trying to catch a market reversal. And so with the crude oil trade, once it had traded above the moving averages I had on my chart, the path of least resistance was for it to go higher still. There was no need to start looking at shorting a reversal because the trend was so strong to the long side.

The price on the chart was making higher lows and higher highs. These are the characteristics of an uptrend. The price structure of a downtrending market is that you would see the price making lower lows and lower highs. In this case, crude oil was on a very strong uptrend and entering and exiting trades was all about the timing.

I like to see the moving averages on the chart supporting price. You tend to get stronger trends when they line up in order. So I like to see the short-term moving average first (the 8EMA), then the 20EMA, then the 50EMA, and finally the big 200EMA all in line. When I see that they are sitting underneath the latest price candlestick in this order, then I am looking for a healthy trending market to the long side.

These signals showed me that crude oil was trending higher so I started swing trading it to the long side, but I was also day trading some positions. I started day trading on a five-minute chart, which meant I was watching what the price did every five minutes and adjusted my position accordingly. I would make some money and bank it, then adjust my stop loss and stay in the trade in a no-lose position that I could hold for a week or so, i.e. keeping my stop loss above my original entry point, guaranteeing me a profit, no matter what happened from that point on.

I would leave some of my position on the table overnight and, more often than not, I would wake up the next morning, log on to my computer, and find I had made money overnight. Even if I didn't make much, even if I'd automatically been closed out of the trade by my stop loss, I was protected against losing money because my stop loss order was above my entry on the trade.

It was such a volatile market and I had such extensive experience of trading with this strategy that I ended up making a pretty decent amount of money in a relatively short space of time. It was a clear and simple strategy and I stuck to it religiously.

This simple strategy, to build a position whilst managing my risk at all times, has always worked for me so I apply it to most of my trading. Plus, it works hand in hand with my belief that being in the GMT time zone gives us the best advantage. Being sandwiched between the US and the Australasian markets is the most advantageous position to be in, in my opinion. The markets push prices when they open in what is the middle of the night in Europe, so by the time we wake up, we're able to catch the end of that trend after a night of price movement.

If we leave some positions open at the end of the day, we can make money as the US market opens and keeps the ball in the air, continuing to drive prices up. Then, as the US is closing, the Asian session is getting ready to open again. By the time we're on our second coffee in London and the LSE is opening again, we're catching the end of the Asian session again and the whole cycle starts over. In the industry this is called the London Fix.

As I became more and more fascinated by crude oil, I got excited about the key benchmarks that stood to be hit. I remember the day the price of crude oil went over $100 a barrel. The market went wild. Then the press started saying that it would never hit the $150 mark, but my indicators were telling me a different story, it was telling me that there was going to be no let up in the bullish trend we were experiencing. I kept my positions open, according to what my signals told me to do.

Finally, in the middle of 2008, the price of crude oil hit a historic high of $147. I was excited to watch it happen and see my signals proved right. I'd successfully followed a trend and applied a strategy that made me a sizeable profit out of this volatile market.

I now see myself as a bit of a crude oil expert, particularly as a day trader. I know when to go long and I know when to short it. If you can get that balance right, there is considerable money to be made.

Unlike gold or silver, crude oil is an essential commodity that is internationally sought-after on a constant basis. The same applies to the grains market, another one of my favourite markets to trade. Huge global demand means hugely fluctuating prices, and thus big potential profits from the price movements, if you know what you are doing.

As I said before, and as I always tell my students, if you can learn to trade the crude oil market successfully, I believe you can trade anything.

CHAPTER SEVENTEEN:
GOLD

Finding the top of the gold market

WHILE NEVER MOVING with anything like the volatility of the crude oil market, gold is a commodity that also experienced a bullish market in the latter part of the last decade. The trend was, in part, driven by the financial crisis. People buy gold to protect their assets in times of financial dislocation.

When the economy becomes unstable, people pull their money out of risk appetite markets such as stocks and move it into safe markets like bonds, gold and the US dollar. Investors get smaller returns but have the reassurance that their money is safe. Indeed, you can't really get safer than the bond market, as bonds are guaranteed by their respective governments.

Once upon a time, gold was a currency. Everything was bought with gold, or a representation of it; all money used to be fixed on a gold standard. No country currently uses a gold standard because it was shown to limit economic growth (although this remains a controversial topic because being off the gold standard is also linked to inflation). Many countries, nevertheless, still hold gold reserves.

The UK had huge gold reserves until Gordon Brown, then Chancellor of the Exchequer, decided to sell them. He did it, for some unknown reason, when the price of gold was at an all-time low. Between 1999 and 2002, Brown sold off around 60% of Britain's gold reserves. Shortly after this time, the price of gold quadrupled in price. It was a highly controversial move that seemed to baffle many top economists and angered British taxpayers. He effectively made a really bad trade.

It's a shame Gordon hadn't studied at Trading College. He could have made billions – if not trillions – more if he'd followed the right signals on a good chart package and had got his timing right.

The chart below shows the gold price from 2005 to late 2013.

Gold price over the last five to six years

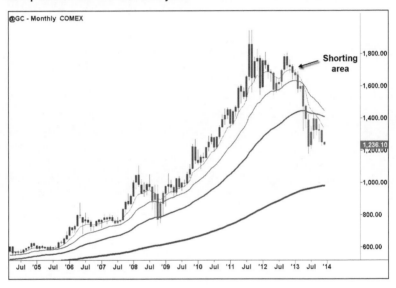

Throughout the first decade of the 21st century, there was a constant uptrend in the price of gold, with a slight correction in 2008 (which means that the price stopped moving up and moved down for a short period of time before it returned to an uptrend again).

In January 2009, I was tracking gold on my Pro-Trading System and I got a signal to buy. This was shown by the appearance of a green candlestick after a series of red ones. I could see we were starting to get higher lows and higher highs in price, which confirmed the signal, so I got into the trade. Remember, when we see this on a chart we could see a very healthy bull market starting and this was certainly what happened with gold. When you see the potential of a very big move coming, it's a little hard not to start dreaming about the big profits rolling in.

It was a good trade but before long, everyone started to get in on the act. Gold shops were opening up everywhere to buy and sell gold, and Angela Rippon hosted a TV documentary about why we should all start buying gold – we were getting to the point of what I call "taxi driver syndrome".

With all due respect to taxi drivers, when they are starting to talk to all their passengers about a certain market being a good one to get into, I know it means the price is about to collapse. This is the point at which I usually start getting signals to short that particular market.

To some extent, this feeds into a strategy that professional traders play to their great advantage. They get into their long positions and start driving prices up with lots of 'word on the street' hype and press releases. Just when the general public starts to get into the market, the professionals sell their positions at the top of the market. When the uneducated public enters a market, it is usually time to sell and get out, or to go short. I've seen this happen so many times and it irritates me because the man on the street loses out whilst the same old bankers make a killing. The public buy at the top of the market, the prices start to fall, and the public lose out while the professional traders pocket the profit.

If you are ever sitting in the back of a cab and the driver starts talking about a top investment tip he's just got, watch carefully how that particular stock or market starts behaving. You can be pretty sure it's the end of a cycle and the prices are about to start falling. In fact, if you want, you can trade it.

On 22 August 2011 gold hit a new record high of just over $1900, after which it started to come down slowly. Then prices started to increase again in 2012. As they started to move up for a second time, the people who missed the first climb scrambled to get into the trade.

However, in October 2012, even though the long signals from my PTS were still valid, I could see a major red flag in the monthly chart, indicating that the end of this bull market for gold was around the corner (for more information on my PTS, see 'My Pro-Trading System (PTS)' on page 142). As I've explained before, I like to place trades with the moving averages underneath the candlesticks. At this point, I knew there was a healthy trending market, but there comes a time when the buyers of any market start to dry up and a drop in price is inevitable.

The price on a chart moves in waves and there are only a certain amount of buying waves until the buyers start to turn into sellers and the price drops. What happens at the top of any market is that there is no one left to buy and push the price up. Unfortunately this is the point at which the public tend to enter the market and get hurt because the price has peaked. By the time news of any commodity or stock reaching record historic highs hits the headlines, professional traders are heading for the door and banking their profitable trades. This is what was happening with gold in 2012. I knew the buying wave patterns were coming to an end on the monthly charts and a multi-year high in gold was setting up.

As soon as the price of gold broke below $1706 I got into a longer-term short trade in gold and decided to sit on the trade until the next price support area on the chart, which was around $1560. That was a big move and I was prepared to trade it down to that level. Fellow traders in my live trading room thought I was crazy. They were getting the same signals as me but because of what they were hearing in the news, they were certain the price of gold was still in a long uptrend. So they stayed in long positions. The price held fairly steady for months. I stood my ground despite all my co-traders continuing to tell me I was nuts. They continued to go long. They couldn't believe what I was doing.

It was a huge test of patience, even though I had employed my usual risk strategy, and I had to get comfortable with how much I could lose if the trade went against me. But it paid off! Finally, the price of gold started to fall and I started to cash in. My signals had been correct and I had successfully found the top of the gold market. Eventually the price dropped even further then $1560 (at the time of writing, it is down to around the $1200 area).

I wish I could tell you I was still in my short trade, but I got out around that $1560 mark. It's very common to hear traders say, 'I wish I was still in that trade'. On the other hand, I exited the trade when I did because I wanted to walk away with a nice profit. For all I knew the price could have turned again and I could have lost all my profits. I'm happy with what I walked away with.

This is a great example of how if you make the right choices on whether to go long or to short the market, at the right time, you can make money in any market that is moving in any direction. You just have to employ the right strategy and stick to the plan.

CHAPTER EIGHTEEN:

APPLE

Finding the top of Apple shares

MY EXPERIENCE WITH the gold market is not unlike the experience I had with Apple shares.

I hadn't paid Apple a huge amount of attention during my trading career, but in September 2012 I noticed that Apple shares were in a particularly bullish trend. Word on the street was that this would continue, indefinitely. However, I was getting a bearish dynamic divergence signal from my MACD indicator on my chart, which told me that the price was about to collapse. I subsequently put out a newsletter to my Trading College members saying that I was bearish on Apple, which was contrary to popular belief.

Then I started receiving emails from investors I'd never heard from before telling me I was out of my mind. No one expected Apple to do anything but continue its upward trend. Most of these people were fundamental traders and based on their fundamental analysis Apple was going nowhere except sky high. It was all over CNN and Bloomberg; all the experts were talking about how bullish Apple was, about how high the price was going to go, about how it would probably hit $1000 before the end of the year. They were convinced of it.

But I'm a technical analysis trader and I was getting told a different story. My charts told me that there was a major divergence in the price of Apple shares around the $700 mark (i.e. that there was going to be a massive drop just around this point). Although, of course, I couldn't tell exactly when that would be.

On 21 September 2012, the price of Apple shares hit $705 and I got into a short position based on my signals. The signals were right; the price had peaked at $705 and after that started to plummet. In March 2013, the price of Apple shares hit $495, less than half the expected $1000.

My fellow traders were flummoxed. They had chosen to base their decisions on popular opinion and fundamental analysis. Even though they were technical analysis traders, and their charts were telling them the same story as mine, they had made a different choice. They didn't stick to the plan.

It was tough, believing a technical analysis indicator over what the press was saying, and what other traders were saying, and what strong public opinion was saying, on such a high profile stock, but I stuck to my guns and it paid off. I trusted my plan. I didn't deviate from my strategy. This experience only served to reinforce my determination to trust the signals on my charts.

Some of the lucky investors who bought into Apple right at the beginning have become multi-millionaires thanks to the monumental success of the company. They profited from a buy and hold strategy. But when this strategy is not appropriate for market conditions – when markets are too volatile – it's much safer to preserve your capital and not trade. We can't trade the markets we'd like to have (steadily climbing markets); we can only trade the markets we have. We must use a strategy that works in highly volatile markets.

CHAPTER NINETEEN:

FACEBOOK

The Facebook IPO fiasco

IT WAS LIKE waiting for the second coming in the time before Facebook went public. I have never seen anything so hyped up. It was almost embarrassing to watch.

The initial public offering (IPO) was set for 21 May 2012 and in the days running up to it, it was like the Oscars, the Grammies, the Olympics and Queen's Jubilee all rolled into one. On Bloomberg it was like Christmas in a big department store, with the champagne lined up and every festivity you could imagine being planned. You would have thought no company in history had ever gone public before. But I *had* seen it all before.

In 1997, while I was playing for Sheffield United, the club was floated on the stock market. Ahead of the event, everyone was excited, but I was a little apprehensive. There was a big buzz and people were constantly talking about how much they were going to make. I felt the whole thing had been over-hyped so I decided not to buy any shares, but my dad did, as did many of my mates.

In the first few days the share price went up as expected, but it wasn't long before the price dropped sharply and people lost a lot of money on their initial investment. This experience made me extremely wary of anything being hyped that much.

Basically whenever there's a big buzz about something, and everyone starts talking about what a fantastic investment it's going to be, I start to get wary. I get a hunch it's all going to end in tears.

My first clue that something is getting blown up by media hype is when I start getting calls from non-trader friends telling me they are considering investing in something and asking my opinion. When I start to get those calls, I'm pretty sure I'm going to hold back.

Anyone who called me during that period, to ask whether or not they should buy Facebook shares, got the same answer. I told them I had decided not to buy them because I wasn't convinced it was going to be the great, fast-moving investment everyone was expecting. I only ever tell people what I am going to do, I never tell them what to do; they have to make their decisions. Sometimes I'm right, sometimes I'm wrong. On this one I was right.

The first aspect of the debacle was a fiasco with orders not being properly processed on the NASDAQ exchange. I'm still not sure exactly what went on there, but clearly the system wasn't firing on all cylinders and there were major administrative problems; maybe it was caused by the volume of orders being processed. Whatever actually happened, it was certainly a bad omen.

Facebook shares opened at $36.53; then they immediately started to go down. The price didn't stop falling until 4 September 2012, when it bottomed out at $17.55. It has been steadily climbing since then, and by March 2013 had reached around $27, but anyone who invested at the original offering price is facing a tough decision. Do they get their money out and take the loss now, or do they sit on it and stay in the trade in the long term, hoping they will one day get into profit? If they stay in, they are being forced to hold on to a losing trade. Who knows if the price will ever get back up to the $36 mark again? Facebook once seemed infallible, but social media sites like Twitter and Pinterest seem to be catching up in popularity; it's a rapidly evolving, fickle industry.

The story was very much a sign of the times. There was once a time when you did jump on the bandwagon, when it seemed there was such a thing as a safe bet. I remember when huge companies like British Telecom and Abbey National went public in the 1990s. Most of us invested, or know people who invested in these companies, and held on to shares for the long term, taking a regular, decent-sized dividend along the way; back then you knew certain companies would never falter. Then Northern Rock happened and it's as if the world has never looked back.

It wasn't even as if I was so sure Facebook would fail that I was prepared to short it. I simply didn't know what was going to happen. To be honest, I didn't want to touch it with a barge pole. I bet some people were short on it; I'm sure some people made money.

So here's my advice: the next time you hear about some investment or other being a safe bet and the next big thing, assume the opposite. Or at the very least do your own research.

CHAPTER TWENTY:
RBS

Banking crisis

THE FINANCIAL CRISIS of 2007-2008 that shook the world, the aftershocks of which are still reverberating today, is widely believed to have been kick-started, or at least hugely exacerbated, by the creation of the subprime mortgage market in the US.

What really differentiates this last crisis from the Great Depression precipitated by the Wall Street Crash of 1929 is that people really had no clue what was going on behind the scenes. With hindsight, it is easy to see how margin buying (people buying on credit) artificially inflated the US stock market in the 1920s, which led to the stock market bubble bursting.

To some extent that is what went on during the first decade of the 21st century too, although with property. There have been other property bubbles but this one was made much more serious by one big mitigating factor – banks and other lending institutions were trading mortgage bundles for huge amounts of money despite the fact that these mortgages were hardly worth the paper they were printed on. People had *no idea* that this was going on.

Millions of US homeowners had been sold mortgages that were, or would become, beyond their means, and that were often at 100% of their home's value in an inflated market. When the housing bubble burst, many people were unable to refinance to ease mortgage payments, or found themselves in a position of having negative equity in their homes, meaning that their homes were actually worth less than what they owed on them, and banks came after them for the difference. When people couldn't pay back their loans, because so much had been secured on them, the collapse in the subprime mortgage market effectively destabilised the entire global economy.

The banks were getting into debt that began spiralling out of control, with some literally drowning in debt, to the point at which they had to ask to be bailed out, first by other banks and eventually by their governments.

Of course debt begets debt and after a while it became clear that the worst hit institutions were not actually going to survive. Many small banks had to be bought up by larger banks. This was alarming enough, but when the big banks started going to the wall, the panic really set in. By the time the huge investment banks Merrill Lynch, Bear Sterns and Lehman Brothers went under, the writing was on the wall, and when the US government had to take over the mortgage lenders, Fannie Mae and Freddie Mac, we wondered where on earth it could end.

The situation in the United States was reflected in Britain. In 2007 the British bank Northern Rock found itself unable to pay back loans from the international money market and had to go cap in hand to the government. When this news got out, Britain witnessed its first bank run in over 150 years. There were people queuing around the block to take their money out and some branches started to close their doors. Other UK banks and building societies followed suit. Alliance & Leicester and Bradford & Bingley were amongst the larger institutions to go under.

While the government guaranteed the value of people's Northern Rock bank accounts, it couldn't guarantee the value of Northern Rock shares, and the share price soon began to nosedive. It was around this time that I started getting calls from well-meaning friends telling me I should buy Northern Rock shares, on the assumption that what goes down will eventually come back up. Unfortunately for anyone who did think that they could make a long-term killing on buying Northern Rock shares at a very low value, this proved to be a false assumption; many people lost their entire investment.

Having already seen what happened with Northern Rock, when other banks started going the same way anyone who was an experienced swing trader knew what to do in order to make money out of the situation. We started shorting the banks.

Shorting RBS

I had been following the share price of RBS (the Royal Bank of Scotland) for many years. When I'd started investing in properties in the mid 1990s, I took out most of my mortgages and home loans with RBS, so I'd always had an interest in following the bank. I was aware of how exposed they were to the housing market, so I knew when property prices started to fall they were going to be affected.

In addition, fundamental research confirmed that the banks, in general, were in trouble. I knew there was going to be a good opportunity to short RBS; it was just a case of waiting for an entry point. It happened in May 2007, when the price closed below the 200-day Exponential Moving Average.

RBS shares had spiked through £6 on 23 February 2007, which created a huge double top in the markets. A double top is when price comes back to re-test a previous high price point. This can, and mostly does, prevent prices from going higher. Because traders thought the price was overvalued at £6 before it is very likely they will sell again at £6 when the price reaches this point for the second time. This was once again brought to my attention by my dynamic divergence strategy that works so well on overvalued and undervalued markets.

My entry point was when the price closed below the 200-day Exponential Moving Average in May 2007. The share price (having been up as high as around £6.20) was about £5.40 when I got into the trade in a short position.

At the time, of course, I didn't know how long I was going to be in the trade. Like any other trader who bases their decisions on technical analysis, I waited for the signal to tell me to get out of the trade, to alert me that the dip was over and the share price was about to go up. I waited and waited, and no signal came; the price just kept dropping and dropping.

I kept moving my stop loss down as I made money, locking in the profit. I followed my strategy of banking some profit, keeping a position and then moving my stop loss. Still the price kept going down. I didn't come out of the trade until the share price was only a fraction of what it had started at. I had made a small fortune.

In 2009, the price of RBS shares hit £1. At the time of writing, they are back up to about £3. The share price lost over £6 in a matter of months, which is a great example of just how dramatic the banking crisis was. That is why spread betting became such a lucrative vehicle during this time – traditional long-term investing didn't make sense any more. You couldn't even guarantee that a bank could hold its value.

No one knew how long the crisis was going to last; if we could predict the future like that, we'd all be billionaires. It was like there was a crack in the wall. The government was busy patching it up, but what they couldn't see was that the crack was the tip of the iceberg, a small visible chink, and that behind the wall the entire thing was about to collapse. No one knew how bad it was going to be until after the event, and we are still reeling from it.

At the time, being in the trade wasn't fun. It was scary. It was like being on a log flume in the dark and not knowing when you were going to hit the water and, when you did, whether you were going to get soaking wet or be one of the lucky ones who avoided the big splash.

It was also a bad, bad time. People were getting hurt. People who had money but didn't really understand economics at a higher level were panicking. I remember driving past a long line of people queuing around the block outside the Northern Rock branch in Kingston-upon-Thames and seeing pensioners who were clearly worried sick and had waited for hours in the rain, desperate to get their life's savings out of the bank. They were terrified they were going to lose the lot; they were cursing themselves for not listening to their Victorian grannies who warned them that the only safe place for your money is in the stuffing of your mattress.

Banks had traditionally been *the* safe long-term investment. It was the biggest shake up in the world of finance and investing that anyone had ever experienced. Northern Rock shares stopped trading in 2008, at 0.9p, basically zero. No one could ever have imagined that the value of a bank could drop to nothing. When the building society Abbey National had been floated on the LSE in 1989, almost 2m people bought shares at around £1.30 a share as a long-term investment. Those shares peaked at just over £14 in 2000 before they started a slow and painful decline.

Many technical analysis swing traders were shorting the banks during this period. What else could we do?

The market became extremely volatile. Volatility usually happens when shares are going down. If there are no buyers, investors get desperate, trying to sell off their shares as quickly as possibly. Then the bottom simply falls out of the market. This was all great if you were in a short position, but it was extremely painful for anyone in a long position.

The government bans shorting banks in 2008

At some point the government saw what was going on. They realised that while people could make money on the falling share price of banking stocks, there was no motivation or incentive for the market to recover. They had to stimulate buyers to get back into the market. People couldn't be allowed to sell indefinitely, so they made it illegal to short the banks.

Traders got around it. We started trading other markets and vehicles that move in the opposite direction when bank shares start going down. We got into long positions on these markets so that, while the banks were still falling we could make money, but without actually perpetuating the damage. In this scenario, no banks were being directly harmed, so it wasn't unethical.

There are so many derivative products these days you can always find a product that moves in the opposite direction to a counterpart. It's like the money markets are made up of a series of a seesaws, working against each other.

These correlations have always existed – when the dollar goes down, gold goes up; when interest rates go down the stock market normally goes up – but since the explosion of derivatives, you can now find conversely corresponding products for almost anything you can imagine.

CHAPTER TWENTY-ONE:
GBPUSD

Shorting GBP against USD for 1000 pips profit

I HAVE BEEN trading the forex market for some time. While I've had a number of successful trades in several currency pairs, for a long time I always seemed to get a dose of bad luck when it came to trading the British pound against the US dollar. I'd been in one trade that actually lost me a fair bit of money (although still within my risk parameters) and another that made me a relatively small amount compared to what I'd been hoping for.

Here's where I want to show you how important it is not to let past disappointments change your trading strategy. At the beginning of 2013, I got a bearish signal from my Divergence Strategy telling me to get into a GBPUSD trade in a short position because the pound was weakening against the dollar. (See chart below.) I took my entry once the price broke below a major trend line. The price had bounced off this support trend line several times, but now it had the strength to break below. The bears were winning the battle.

GBPUSD

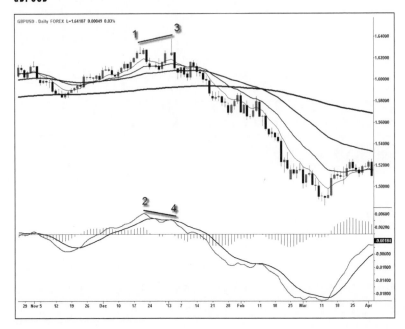

The signal I was getting from my MACD indicator was supported by another signal I got from my PTS. I got a red candlestick following a run of green ones, telling me more sellers were entering the market at a time when the price was optimal to enter the trade.

So I had two of my strategies confirming that it was a good time to enter the trade. However, I'd had a bad experience with the GBPUSD in the past. I'd lost money in this market. I could have easily got gun shy and let my past experiences outweigh what my trading strategies were telling me to do. In the event, I didn't lose my nerve. I went with what I was seeing rather with what I was feeling. I stuck to the plan; I obeyed the signal that told me to get into the trade. And this time it worked out well.

The important thing to note here is that I got into the trade despite my previous experiences. Had I let my past two experiences hold me back, had I not pulled the trigger, I wouldn't have got into a GBPUSD trade for a third time. If I had let the emotions of my past disappointments rule my actions, maybe I would have risked less on the trade.

But I didn't do anything differently. I applied the exact same trading strategy as I always do. I got into the trade when my signals told me to get into it, I risked 3% of my account and I set my stop loss at the corresponding number of pips away from my entry point.

Remember, I only had money to trade with because I'd stuck to my risk strategy the first time. If I'd risked more than my usual percentage on that first GBPUSD losing trade, I could have lost all my money, but because I employed the same risk strategy I always employ, I had only lost 3% of my total capital the previous time.

When I saw the signal and got into this trade, I called it out in my live trading room. I run a live trading room for signed-up students three times a week where I project my screens via a webinar so that they can watch how I am managing my trades and copy me if they want. Anyone who followed me on this trade was about to have a very nice payday, assuming they put the right risk management in place, because the pound went on to move 1000 pips against the US dollar.

I got into the trade on 17 January 2013, when the pound was at around 1.6050 against the dollar. On 13 March, it was down to 1.4924. In less than two months it had moved over 1000 pips. On this trade let's say I traded at £3 per pip on the pound going down against the dollar, entering the trade when the pound was at 1.6050. If my pot is £5000 then my total risk for the trade of 3% must be £150. I set my stop loss at 50 pips above my entry point, at 1.6100. I had to hope that the pound wouldn't suddenly go up to 1.6105, or I'd be stopped out of the trade for a loss of £150.

Once I had opened the trade the pound did go down against the dollar and quite considerably. By the time it had reached 1.5050, I had made £3000 (£3 x 1000 pips). Not a bad sum of money to make in two months, and completely tax-free.

CHAPTER TWENTY-TWO:
LOSING ON AN UPTREND

Shorting the stock market in an uptrend in 2013

IN FEBRUARY 2013, I got a Bearish signal from my Dynamic Divergence system using my MACD indicator (i.e. the MACD line was going down while the price was going up). This told me I should enter a trade in the S&P 500 Index in a short position.

The S&P 500 Index had been steadily rising for some time. My indicator system was predicting it had reached its limit; that it had been stretched out as far as it would likely go and would soon snap back, just like an elastic band if it is stretched out as far as it can go. I got into a short position on the Mini Dow Futures market, expecting to see a downturn.

But the S&P 500 kept rising and rising, very slowly. This was frustrating because it was not because people were buying stocks; it was because the Fed was propping up the market. Indeed, it was rising on very low trading volumes. It's very boring to trade a market that's moving on low volumes; it reduces the range of volatility.

Basically, the Fed was falsely stimulating the market to keep it going up. The market was what is called overbought. The elastic band wasn't snapping back, it was just being stretched a tiny bit more, every day.

In the end, I reached my maximum risk and got stopped out of the trade before the downturn occurred. It's very frustrating knowing that a trend is being falsely eked out instead of taking its natural course. Technical analysis can't account for any anomalous actions taken by the Fed. The market was long overdue a correction, but it just didn't come. I lost money on that trade.

This is an example of how your indicators can't get it right every time. It can't account for mitigating factors; it can only calculate what's likely to happen based on past trends. So sometimes you can follow your plan and do all the right things and you still lose on the trade.

At the beginning of 2013, when I got into the trade, the stock market was seriously over valued. Thank you, Ben! (That's Ben Bernanke, former Chairman of the US Federal Reserve.) I kept asking myself who could be still buying at such extended prices. I'd seen it happen before, at the top of the property market. I'd sold properties to people who were buying at inflated prices, so I knew people like this were out there.

The Fed was printing more and more money to stimulate the economy. At the time of writing at the end of March 2013 the stock market is almost back up to the level it crashed from in 2008. I hope the public aren't going to dive in at these extended prices and get burnt again.

CHAPTER TWENTY-THREE:
MORE TRADING STORIES

The following are more examples of trades where I used my Dynamic Divergence strategy or my PTS strategy to make my decisions.

Trade one: Making 1000 pips profit

I'M LOOKING FOR a wave pattern that ends trends. The end of a trend normally comes with a divergence. The bearish signal is when the price on the chart makes a new high but your MACD indicator that you have on the bottom of your charts does not. In this case there is a high probability that the price is going to come down. Bullish divergence is when the price makes a new low but the momentum indicator you have at the bottom of your chart does not. In this case there is a high probability that price will go up.

The following trade made me nearly a 1000 pips profit and this was included in the trade alerts I send out to the members of Trading College.

As shown on the GBPUSD chart below, on 19 December 2012 the price makes a new high at 1.6306 (1) and so do the MACD indicator lines (2). I'm more interested in the lines on the MACD. On 2 January the previous high of 1.6306 is broken and the price reaches 1.6380 (3), but if you look below at the lines on the MACD (4) they have not made a new high from where the previous high was made. The MACD lines show the strength of the price movements above. This was my heads up that the price would fall on the GBPUSD. How far it would fall, I didn't know. Nor did I know when it would fall.

I actually got into this trade a little later than I would have liked to. My entry was a break below 1.6000 at 1.5998 (5). The reason I placed a trade to short the GBPUSD at that price was because it was a breakout below a big key number (1.6000). Price had also broken a major trend line going back several months. This was all bearish action and I knew a big move was underway now. My stop loss on this trade was at 1.6153.

I knew this trend could last for months and my 1000 pips profit target was sent out several times on my alert service. If you think you're going to get a big move in a trade then you have to learn to sit on your hands and do nothing except manage the trade and trail your stop loss order to lock in your profits.

The 1.5000 profit target was such a big psychological area I was confident that it would be reached. There were several waves up at the end of January and at the start of February I saw my profit go down, but this didn't faze me as there were major moving averages acting as resistance. Once price got down to the 1.5000 area (6) I closed my short position for nearly 1000 pips of profit.

GBPUSD

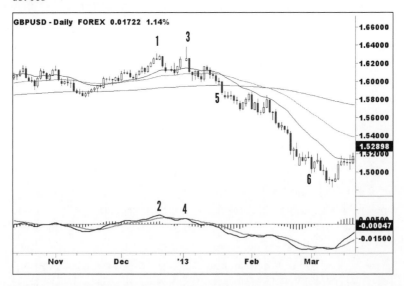

Trade two: major divergence signal in S&P 500

A few years before the trade I described above, on which I lost money in 2013, there was another major divergence in the S&P 500. It happened in 2007. At the time it wasn't known that this was happening just ahead of the biggest economic disaster of a generation.

The weekly chart was presenting a major bearish divergence (1); the MACD was moving down while price was moving up. This told me that it was time to take a trade in a short position. I soon started to make money in this trade.

The stock markets around the world started collapsing. The extent of what was unfolding was only realised later as it began to be reported in the press. The bearish divergence pattern that I had seen on my chart had sparked the decline in the major stock market indices. The end of the uptrend had started. The end of the boom had arrived. The public had no idea what was going to happen next.

What happened was that the price of the S&P 500 halved in two years, people's investments halved in value and there were many horror stories of people losing their properties.

Here is a little tip you may like to take on board: if you see a major divergence signal on a chart and it's confirmed with fundamental news then the reversal could mean a big trade. Sit on your hands and let the trade play out.

In 2009, the S&P 500 bottomed out at around 600 and in July 2013 it was trading at 1636. The chart pattern that started the push higher in stocks in 2009 was bullish divergence – the same pattern that started the crash, except bullish rather than bearish. This pattern is so simple but very powerful.

S&P 500 weekly chart

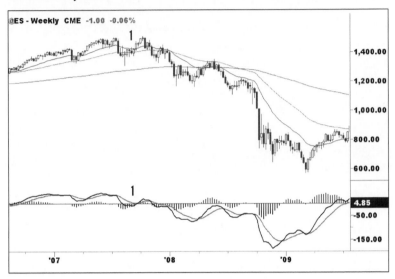

Trade three: EURJPY trade

During the second half of 2011, EURJPY had fallen hard for several months and at some point the market would have to reverse. However, I knew I had to wait for a trigger to tell me the best time to get into the trade – there were some big profits to be made if I entered the trade at the right time.

I was watching the weekly chart and eventually, during the week of 16 December 2011, there was a new low in the market at the same time as I saw the bullish dynamic divergence pattern on the chart. The MACD was moving up while price was still moving down. This told me it was time to get into the trade in a long position. The trigger was the price break above the previous week's high price.

My first entry was at 100.63 (1) with my stop at 96.97 (2). This was a bigger stop distance than I normally feel comfortable with so I had to adjust my position size to allow me to sleep at night. If you're trading any of the yen pairs while you are based in the UK, you have to remember that they are very active overnight UK time, so you could wake up with a significant loss if you don't get the position size of the trade right.

Once I was into the next week of this trade, I decided to move my stop loss up to 98.67 to protect my account, realising that any wild swings lower on price could stop me out before the big push up happened.

In fact, this happened during the following week when the price did indeed come down and reached my stop loss. I took a loss of 196 pips. I was a little disappointed because I know that I have to give these divergence trades room to play out. I also knew that the bullish divergence signal was still there and on 27 July the price made another new low while the MACD did not (3).

It was time to take the trade again. My entry on this trade was 97.33 with a stop loss order at 94.09. Once again, this was a big stop loss distance. It was on a weekly chart and the swings can be big, but so can the rewards. You only need one or two of these trades a year to make a very nice living.

Now I had the trade moving in my favour. The price was moving into the moving averages from below so they were acting as resistance (4). If price consolidates around these moving averages and doesn't sell off again, there is a chance of breaking through and having a big move. This is what happened – price consolidated and then broke through. This was a fantastic result.

I continued to trail my two-bar stop loss order up to lock in the profits and finally exited at 121.15 (5). It was a highly profitable trade. This is an example of how well things can work out when you stick to your plan and strategy.

EURJPY

Trade four: EURAUD trade

Remember that weekly divergence signals are very powerful and could change the direction of a trend that could last for years.

The divergence signal shown in the EURAUD chart below was an instance just like this. It was similar to the time I scored a goal in the last minute of a game, making the score 1-0; it's a game changer.

EURAUD had put in a bottom on 10 February 2012 (1). There was then a new low price on 3 August 2013 (3). If you look closely, you can see that the MACD for those two dates is nearly at the same level at (2) and (4). Even though the MACD at the two dates is very close together, the price on the chart is significantly lower on 3 August than on 10 February. I was seeing the trend to the downside losing its momentum and expecting there would soon be a push higher.

This was the time to take a trade. If you see a big difference in the new low price compared to the last low price, but the MACD lines are very much at the same level, momentum is shifting. The divergence signal and the final wave down was the bottom of the EURAUD for a year. However, I didn't get greedy and exited the trade for over 400 pips profit.

EURAUD

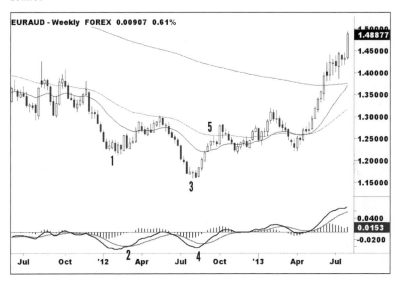

Trade five: In and out of USDCAD in a day

Here's an example of a trade that I took during one day, looking to make a profit overnight. The trade is taken from 240-minute charts, which are a good place to start day trading from. The signal again was a divergence; the price is going to come down. So I placed my trade on day one (1) expecting to be in profit on the trade on day two (2), then I would close it down for a profit. It was a 24-hour trade. It wasn't all that exciting, but generated enough of a profit to buy an appetiser in one of Gordon Ramsay's restaurants!

Divergence was the name of the game for this trade. I entered the trade at 1.0585 with a stop 40 pips away. The price did continue higher after

I entered the trade but it didn't reach my stop loss order, so I didn't get stopped out. The next day I woke up and the trade was in profit. I closed this trade out straightaway for a 34 pip profit because that was my plan.

I like to refer to this as "making money while you sleep."

USDCAD

Trade six: trading crude oil

I really do enjoy trading crude oil but as I have said before it can be a dangerous market to trade. If you are new to trading, you should give it a wide berth.

This was another "make money while you sleep" trade, using the divergence wave patterns. Crude oil had been range-bound for several months, but with tensions running high in Egypt the price took off and went from $93 to $103 in about 11 trading days (1). However, on a 240-minute chart there was a major bearish divergence and the price was due a move lower (2). How far I wasn't sure, but I was prepared to take the trade.

There was another issue with this trade and that was the fact that the divergence signal came on a Friday and we were hearing reports that the Suez Canal was being blocked and that this might prevent the oil tankers from getting through. Was I going to take this trade and miss out on some potential profits or was I going to stand aside?

When anyone asks me this question, my instinct is to say that the best thing to do is to stand aside and not take the trade, to play it safe. But then I put my trading head back on and remember that all my back testing I have done over the years, using charts, is never done knowing what the current news happened to be at the time. I just back test the trade signals on a chart. I don't know whether there was a shock interest rate decision or something like that happening at some particular point in time, I just watch the charts. I decided to take the trade in crude oil.

My entry on this trade was at 103.87 (3) with my stop loss at 104.37. Once again my plan was to close the trade the next trading day. It was now Monday and crude oil was trading lower, as expected, so I closed the trade at 102.20, which was prior to resistance levels that had now become support. Profit on the trade was 167 points.

Crude oil

Trade seven: Goldman Sachs

At the Trading College members' Scan Club that we hold once a week we picked this lovely bearish divergence signal in the US stock, Goldman Sachs. This was on a weekly time frame and it was only a matter of time before there was a move lower on in Goldman's share price. Remember the weekly divergence signals are the most powerful.

The trade triggered the entry with a stop at the very high of the last candlestick. This was a very large stop distance as my entry was 161.07 (1) with a stop loss order at 168.20. That's a 713-point stop distance. If I bought 500 shares in Goldman's, or traded it at £5 per point, my loss would be £3565, a loss I wasn't prepared to take. So I decided to drill down to a smaller time frame to get a precision entry.

I used the daily chart for my entry and stop loss positions. Entry was now 158.62 with a stop loss at 162.26. I could do something with this and get a much larger position size. Goldman traded all the way down to $150 (2), which was a great place to cover my short since $150 is a psychologically important round number.

Goldman Sachs

GS - Weekly NYSE -0.03 -0.02%

Trade nine: No gold for me

This trade on gold didn't play out quite how I wanted it to and I must confess that I broke my rules on this trade. My rules state that for a wave pattern to finish and for a price reversal to occur, the latest price has to be higher or lower than the recent price high or low. Otherwise it is not a divergence.

After picking near enough the top in gold on the monthly chart, I thought gold was in for a push higher. There were MACD lines higher than the previous lows, but what was not present was a price lower than the previous lows (1) and (2). They were $15 apart. This was not a divergence trade in my book. Thinking I was being clever, I decided I would trade it anyway because it was near enough there. However, as I've explained before, unless your rules have been met you shouldn't take a trade.

The price made a new low on 16 April and nearly confirmed a new low on 20 May, but this didn't breach the previous low. Even though the MACD lines were showing a higher low, the trade didn't meet the rules.

I ended up taking this trade at 1398 and spent nearly a month in a sideways market. The price hardly moved and I had money tied up in the trade. This can be really frustrating because that was money that I could have used to enter another trade that might have been making me a profit. I moved my stop up and made a loss on this trade of 11 points. I was disappointed with myself for taking such a poor trade.

Gold

Trade ten: 132 points profit on AUDUSD trade

Not every divergence signal turns into a big reversal trade.

Take a look at the AUDUSD chart below and I'm sure you can see a major wave pattern to the down side, but with a divergence and a potential bottom in this market. On 11 June 2013 there was a new low price and a MACD line higher than the previous low's lines (1). With the divergence signal in place, all I had to do was enter the trade, work out my risk and watch the profits roll in. My entry on this trade was at 0.9471, with my stop at 0.9324. Price did push higher, as expected, and my first profit target was hit at 0.9594 (2).

I like to use prior resistance or support areas for my profit targets and now moved my stop up to just in front of where I entered the trade at 0.9480. I was in a no losing trade. However this was not going to be the big move I had hoped for and the trend soon resumed its move lower and closed me out for a profit. This can and does happen, so you have to just manage your risk on every trade. There is nothing to be gained from trading without a stop loss in place. It's not brave; it's risky.

AUDUSD

Trade eleven: Europe in a mess

Simplicity is essential if you want to trade the markets successfully, which is why I have coded up my own indicators to highlight when one of my trade strategy signals occurs. I have alarms that go off when it's time to trade, giving me the best possible chance of getting into all possible winning trades. I could be making a cup of tea and I hear an alarm go off, at which point I will run back to my screen and place the trade.

I designed the Pro-Divergence to alert me as to when a divergence signal has happened. The indicator sounds an alarm, which prompts me to go to my chart and check the entry price, my stop and the profit target. Once the indicator has done its job, I then just have to place the trade with my broker.

On the weekly chart of the EURUSD below, you can see how between April and July we had a bearish divergence at (1) and (2). All I had to do then was to decide how much I wanted to risk on the trade. As it was a weekly time frame there was the potential to be in this trade for months. The break below the previous week's low was all I needed to realise the market was entering a correction phase. From 1.6000 price collapsed all the way down to 1.2500 (3). I wasn't in this all the way down to 1.2500, as I got out of the trade at the 1.4000 area due to a hammer candlestick that appeared at this level, but it was still a couple of thousand pips profit.

EURUSD

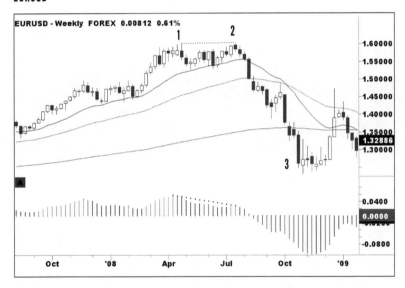

Trade twelve: A trend in EURAUD

EURAUD is a very nice trending FX pair. In April 2012 it started to make a base in the market, at which point I put this pair on my watch list.

I could see there was a drop of around 600 pips in a couple of months but some signs of strength started to be shown in early April (1). However this wasn't a signal to buy EURAUD, as it could have just turned around and continued lower. I wanted to see some more buyers coming into this market and used my indicators to help me see when this happened.

On 8 April there was a push into the 50 and 200 exponential moving averages. These moving averages act as a resistance for any market. However, just by seeing some strength in this market over a week or so and the push into the moving averages was not enough to trigger a buy signal. Remember, I explained earlier that wave patterns alone are not sufficient to act as my buy and sell signals. I wanted to see if it could lead to the completion of an early wave.

The shallow pull back in the price after the push into the moving averages created a bearish dynamic divergence signal. This told me that the sellers might have given up shorting this pair and there could now be a move higher.

In the event, price broke through the major moving averages (3) and at this point I sent a text alert to my members to alert them to the situation. There are other entry points with this trade because it provided several waves. One way is to wait for the break of the moving averages and then buy the pullback to the moving averages because at that point they become support instead of resistance (4).

Just think of these wave patterns as the waves on the beach. Waves go in and out like price goes up and down. EURAUD presented some very nice waves on its move up to 1.4000 from 1.2600. This is a very big move and it all started from that first wave.

EURAUD

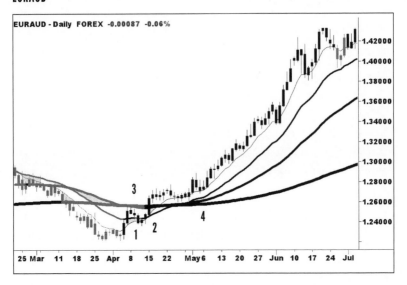

USDJPY

As you can see on the chart below, during the first two weeks of November the PTS broke above the moving averages and the candlesticks changed colour from light (red) to dark (green). This was my buy signal. As the PTS automatically gave me my entry price, stop loss and the projected profit targets, I was all set to enter this trade. The great thing about the PTS is that it automatically generates my position size and my risk reward – all I have to do is wait to receive the audio alert.

Entry price was 80.16 (1), with a stop loss at 79.36. Once I'm committed to the trade all I'm looking for is a light (red) candlestick to tell me to get out of the trade.

In late November and early December, the trade started to go sideways, which wasn't good news for me. This was really going to test my patience. But on 12 December the price exploded higher and broke out of the consolidation. I was delighted with this and from here on it was all about trailing my stop loss order at the price the PTS instructed me to.

Every day I checked to see if the PTS stop loss number had moved up. When it did, I opened my brokerage account and did the same. Sometimes, if I'm away from my screens, I will do this on my iPhone.

From this point, I was locking in more profits every day; I couldn't lose on the trade. On 23 January I got the light (red) candlestick, which was my exit signal (2). I knew it was now time to get out of the trade. In fact my trailing stop loss order did the trick and I was closed out for 88.10. This was a 794-pip profit trade.

USDJPY

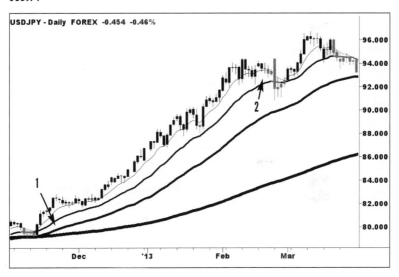

A gift from the trading gods

The chart below shows a US stock called Potash that I was looking at as it had buy-out rumours surrounding it. It was hot stock and many traders were talking about it. However, even when there are rumours and news items about the instrument I'm looking to trade, I will never place a trade unless my system gives me the signal. I'm not trading based on the news; I'm trading based on my system.

I entered this trade at $36.46 (1) at the start of August when the PTS gave me a safe zone area to enter the trade. After I entered the trade, the price consolidated and went sideways. This was fine. As long as the candlesticks didn't turn light (red) I was doing okay in this trade. Two days after I entered the trade, as soon as the US stock markets opened that day, I looked to see where the price on Potash was going to be trading. I was amazed to see it gap up to $48 (2). It felt like a gift from the trading gods. The trade was now in profit over 1000 spread betting points in just a few days. If you had been long on this, with £5 per point, that would have meant £5000 profit in a matter of days. All you had to do to make that money was click a mouse and enter a trade.

So now I'm in profit over 1000 points. What would you have done? Would you sell the trade now and walk away or would you go for more profit? This is a tough question. The greed was kicking in and I wanted to go for more profits, but I already had a very nice profit. Remember though, the profit was not mine until I clicked the mouse and closed the trade. Profits are unrealised until you do this.

Plus, the PTS was still dark (green). I had a decision to make. I decided to bank all the profits and walk away. I closed my PC down and took the rest of the day off. If I had sat there watching my screen and looking at the profits I would have made if I had stayed in the trade, I could have driven myself mad! It was a good profit so I banked it.

In the end, the stock went pretty much sideways for a month and a half after it hit $50.

Chart showing price of US company Potash

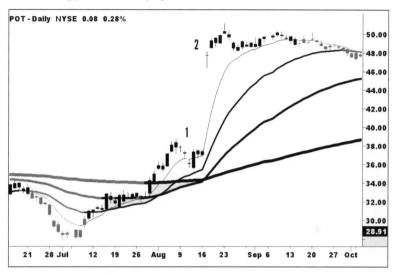

A nice way to book a holiday

I'm the holiday decision maker in the family and I pride myself with being a bit of an expert in finding quality locations that aren't overcrowded. One evening, I got my laptop out, as I always do, to open my charts and see how the US stock markets were going to close. On this particular occasion I decided to have a browse online for our next holiday location.

I was already short the USDJPY chart at 81.96 (1) based on a light-coloured (red) short signal from 11 March 2011. It was a routine new trade signal with a reverse from a dark (green) candlestick to a light (red) one – this being the short signal. The stop on it was 82.84. So I was risking 88 pips on the trade. In the next few days price dropped around 233 pips. This was great but not as great as what happened on the night in question.

All of the stock indices had closed. My partner, Tamasine, had just called out to ask if I would like a coffee. At exactly the same time, the price completely collapsed around 290 pips. I'm short on this trade and now I can see my profit explode in degrees of thousands of pounds (2). Tamasine asked again whether I wanted a coffee. I suddenly realised that I hadn't answered her because I had been concentrating so hard. I told her to hold on while I finished paying for our next holiday. I didn't mention the fact that I meant actually *making* the money for our holiday.

In the space of ten minutes or less, I had paid for our next holiday as well as earning all of our spending money. I could have got even more out of this trade if I'd been a little quicker, but I closed the full position down again as there had been a parabolic move and I didn't want to get greedy. I did go to bed with a huge smile on my face that night, saying a big thank you in my head to the Bank of Japan.

USDJPY

PART FOUR

TRADING IN FOOTBALL TERMS

CHAPTER TWENTY-FOUR:
THE PERFECT GAME MYTH

The Invincibles

IN THE 2003-04 Premier League season, Arsenal won the title without losing a single game. No team had completed a season without losing a game in over 100 years (when football was very different and there were fewer games per season). It will probably be a long time before a team achieves that again. That season's Arsenal team was nicknamed The Invincibles.

Of course Arsenal didn't show up and start playing football yesterday. This is a club that has to date won 13 top league titles and ten FA Cups. In an aggregated league of the entire 20th century, it would be placed first.

Arsène Wenger became Arsenal's manager in 1996. The 2012-13 season was his 17th season with the club. In that time, *including* the 2003-04 season, what percentage of games do you think he won? By January 2013 it was 53.33%.

How's that for a statistic? Arguably the most successful English team, with one of the longest-running managers in the history of the game (only surpassed by Alex Ferguson's 26-year run at Manchester United and just ahead of David Moyes, who spent ten years at Everton), Arsenal won just over half the games it played over the course of 17 years under its longest-serving, legendary, manager.

I try to explain this to people when they show up at my seminars asking me to tell them how they can guarantee making money on every trade. I explain that it is not about winning *every* trade; it's about winning the *majority* of trades. I don't know why people have this notion that being a great trader means winning 100% of their trades. In what other walk of life can you expect to win 100% of the time, especially when you are starting out?

Lose the fear of losing

It's not so much that people want to have all their trades be profitable, it's more about not wanting to *lose* any, because losing money is bad, right? Well, yes. But instead of seeing a losing trade as *losing* money, you could try seeing it as buying you experience.

I've been trading on and off for almost 20 years, and full-time for the last eleven of those. I've worked tirelessly at it. I'm one of the most successful traders I know, but some days I *still* have losing trades. It would be unrealistic to expect otherwise. A good measure of success is how *well* you lose.

The moment I knew I'd turned a corner in trading was when I had a loss and it didn't affect me for a second. I didn't even think about it. I'd had plenty of losses before but for some reason, on this occasion, I didn't view it as losing money, I viewed it as part of the long-term process. I've never looked back.

You need experience to get to that point. Think of every losing trade you have as a small step towards being immune to the effects of losing money. Hopefully that will help you think more positively about your losing trades. When you can lose a trade and it has no effect on you, when you can kiss your money goodbye without batting an eyelid because you know it's part of the bigger picture, *then* you will really start getting somewhere.

There's no difference between me losing £100 and you losing £100. The only thing that differentiates our experiences is how we *respond* to losing that money. If I carry on regardless, immediately forgetting all about it and continuing to trade exactly according to my strategy, then I've lost well. If you get completely depressed about it and it shakes your confidence and affects your decisions, then you've lost badly. In this case, we have had very different experiences.

The difference between Arsenal losing and another team losing is that Arsenal don't let it alter their confidence in their next game. They have a strategy. They play with this strategy and it works, the majority of the time.

Coming close to perfect

There's winning and there's losing. But there's really no such thing as the perfect game. As a footballer, I started out with some talent and I got some good breaks. I worked hard, did the training and saw the results. I played over 500 games in my professional career. How many of those games would I call close to perfect? Two.

That's right. I consider less than 1% of my professional games to have been near-perfect games, and yet I still consider my career to have been a success. Yes, it could have been even better, but I still did extremely well. It wasn't just because I won well – I also lost well.

One of the most important things to grasp when you learn to trade, is how to lose without it destroying your confidence. Losing a trade does not make you bad at trading; everyone loses trades. It's how you respond to it that defines how good a trader you are. If you have a losing trade and as a result you deviate from your set rules, if you stop following your plan, then you are not trading well. If you have that losing trade, that bad experience, and you carry on following your plan and your rules as if nothing happened, then you are trading well.

In his book, *Adapt: Why Success Always Starts With Failure*, the economist Tim Harford explains how we cannot win without first learning to lose, that to make the most out of our experiences and get ahead, we need to fail often but fail small, because without little failures, we are doomed to have bigger ones. This is the most perfect advice for traders. Harford talks about risk, about how there is no success without risk, but how well-planned, calculated risk is the ideal format for success.

While I was playing in those two near-perfect games I just mentioned, it was like being in *the zone*. I remember them like they were yesterday. I've been in the zone both while playing football and while trading. It's a rare experience, but when it happens there's nothing like it. It feels like you're coasting, or flying, with everything just seeming to go exactly to plan.

I mentioned one of those games in the first part of this book. It was the FA Cup semi-final game against Newcastle at Old Trafford, when I got lucky that the ref didn't give me a second yellow card for a messy tackle on Alan Shearer.

I clearly remember the moments before the game, how everything felt like it was going perfectly to plan. I remember noticing that my kit was laid out perfectly, noticing my boots were spotless, feeling the best I'd ever felt after the warm-up, thinking about how my family were all out there, in the crowd, ready to watch me with pride.

When footballers are not playing in their home ground, they try to recreate the exact same conditions at the away ground. Any little rituals are recreated; everything in the changing room is put in the same place, so nothing throws you off. That day, it all felt perfect.

A feeling of total calm descended upon me. As I walked on to the pitch, I didn't feel nervous or excited, I just felt right, as if this was my moment to shine, as if nothing could possibly go wrong, and that I didn't have to do anything to feel that way, it was like it was all effortless. I played the whole game in the same complete state of calm. That's *the zone*.

One moment in particular during this game defined what it was like. It all happened in a matter of seconds. Shearer had the ball and got past me, heading towards the goal. The keeper came out and slid to the ground as he went to grab the ball. Shearer chipped the ball over the keeper and it started to roll into the goal. I lunged forward, stretching my leg out as far as possible and somehow made contact with the ball. I cleared it nicely off the goal line.

The moment came and went as if I was programmed to do it. I didn't think, "I might misjudge the angle and knock it in for an own goal," I didn't think, "I might bring Shearer down and give away a penalty, as well as getting sent off for a second yellow card," both of which were real risks. I just went with my instinct. I trusted that, with my skill and preparation, the risky move would go to plan and work out in my favour. That's exactly what happened.

I look back now and think there was no particular reason why on that day, on that occasion, that particular moment in the game went so smoothly. I couldn't have predicted it. It wasn't predictable but, thanks to my preparation, thanks to the creation of near-perfect conditions, it was probable.

Of course there was still an element of chance that my decision wouldn't have gone the right way. On a different day, the voices of fear might have stopped me from going for it. But that day, in that moment, with everything set up for a successful result, it worked in my favour.

Control what can be controlled

I meet hundreds of people every year who are traders, or want to be traders. Most of them have one thing in common that I feel holds them back significantly. They are all chasing that holy grail. They are all looking for the latest fail-safe system, the newest set of indicators or some never-before-used strategy that will enable them to guarantee success; that will make all their trades winning trades. They are all trying to figure out how to have the perfect game.

I try to explain to them that having the perfect game is out of their control. There is no way to guarantee the perfect game, because you cannot guarantee what the opposition is doing. There is no holy grail, there is no perfect plan. There is only perfect preparation – the rest is chance.

That idea of the perfect trading strategy exists in the mind, along with the perfect football game. You can imagine the perfect football game; in your mind you can control every element of the game, every external factor. But in real life it can't exist because you can't control the other team, you can't control the weather, you can't control what the crowd starts chanting, just like you can't control the markets.

That's why I constantly try to impress upon people that no matter what choices you make, no matter what your top-notch, latest indicator system tells you, no matter what fancy new strategy you adopt, you still can't control what the markets do.

Once you accept that you are playing against the markets and that the markets are real, fluctuating entities that move and change of their own accord, independently from whatever you do in your trading strategy, then you are on a winning path. In fact, if there *is* such a thing as a holy grail it is the acceptance that you have no control over the markets.

The day I fully accepted that no matter what I did, no matter what choices I made, no matter how much I knew, there was absolutely nothing I could do to predict or influence the markets, was the day I felt set free. It is particularly liberating to realise what you are in control of and what you aren't in control of.

You have plenty of factors to worry about; focus on them. Forget about what the markets are doing. Figure out your best strategy, make sure your chart package is accurate and your indicator system works well. Work out your risk strategy; fine-tune your trading plan. Do the things you can control and forget about the things you can't control.

You can't predict the perfect outcome; you can only do everything that is within your control to give yourself the best probable outcome. You can only control your own actions, you cannot control anyone else's. (We could all do with remembering this more often!)

Of course the unpredictability of the markets isn't your only opponent. You have a more ferocious opponent than that.... yourself.

You are your own nemesis in trading. Your fears, your laziness, your indecision, your impatience... are all factors that will play against you. The good news is that at least you can exercise control over these factors. It's not always easy, but it is possible. If you do the work, if you figure out your own mind and know how your emotions work and what kind of past experiences and disappointments are most likely to trip you up, you can control this opponent.

People show up at Trading College to learn about trading with unreal expectations all the time. They want to turn £1000 into a million in a matter of months. That's like showing up at Arsenal having played a little amateur football and expecting to play in their first team and score a hat-trick by the end of the season. You have to learn to manage your expectations.

CHAPTER TWENTY-FIVE:
THE RELEGATION ZONE

Playing like you're not going down

I'VE SEEN TEAMS play some of their best football when they are in danger of being relegated. I've also seen teams play their worst. This is because when you're in the relegation zone you have two choices: either you believe you can still get out of the relegation zone and you focus all your efforts on playing your best, or you give up before the season's over and accept defeat.

How do those teams who get out of the relegation zone do it? By playing like they are not going down. By playing as if they are at the top of the league and believing they are going to be staying there for a long time. By playing as if they expect to win.

In effect, every time you trade, it's like you're in that relegation zone, because there is always a chance of going down, of losing on that trade. If you give up and accept you are going down you won't play well, you will make bad choices. Only by believing you can win will you play your best and make the best choices.

If you play like a second-rate trader, your results will be second rate. Play like a successful trader. Find a successful trader and copy them. Play like they play. As Anthony Robbins, the American life coach, says, "If you want to be successful, find someone who has achieved the results you want and copy what they do and you'll achieve the same results."

All successful traders I know trade with the knowledge that they are good. If you can believe that, too, you can achieve the same results. How do traders become successful? By trading as if they are already successful. They trade as if they are already making a good profit from trading and will continue to do so long term.

Playing without fear

What made me a good defender was that I could read the game well. I could see the risk in and around the penalty box. I never let fear stop me going for the ball; I would just go for it. If I had always hesitated, if I was always thinking about the risks, I never would have made the tackles I did and put my head in where it hurts.

I learnt to play football fearlessly and you have to learn to trade fearlessly. It doesn't matter how many times you lose a trade, it only matters that you win more often than you lose. It's still statistics. You still need to keep on trading every time you see your strategy appear on your chart because you never know when that big winning trade will happen.

In January 2013, I was watching Liverpool play Manchester United at Old Trafford and I noticed Luis Suárez had a particularly bad game. He kept losing control of the ball and he failed to put away a single goal; his touch was terrible. This was because every time he got the ball, the Manchester fans started booing him. Alex Ferguson had made some scathing remarks in the press about Suárez diving and the fans decided to give him a hard time. He let it get under his skin. He let it affect his performance. If only he'd had the mental strength to block it out, he might have scored enough goals to win the game.

Of course that is easier said that done. I'm sure you'd be put off your game if thousands of football fans were booing you every time you touched the ball. But if you want to be a good trader, you better get used to booing, because the markets boo you all the time. You put a trade on and the markets boo you by not doing what you are expecting. Are you going to let that throw you off your game? You had better not, or you won't score any more goals. You have to get experience or you'll never be able to block out those negative factors.

If a goalkeeper allowed the fear of getting hurt or dropping the ball to enter his mind, he'd never go for the ball. That doesn't mean he's never experienced it. Any goalkeeper at the top of his career has dropped or missed the ball a thousand times (most of those in training of course), but those thousand times have been essential in giving him the fearlessness to go for the ball every time. The goalkeepers who don't make it into the top teams are the ones who crumple after the failed saves. The best ones don't let it affect them, or at least don't let it show that they are affected. By being *unafraid* of dropping the ball, a goalkeeper is more likely to catch it.

Think of an ice skater learning to do a jump. Do you think in the course of learning to do a complicated jump they never fall? Of course they fall, they fall several times, and probably more often as the jump gets increasingly difficult. They practice and practice until they can do the jump perfectly, until they are no longer afraid of falling. Once they are no longer afraid of falling, they are less likely to fall.

I have a friend who's a yoga fanatic and she tells me her teacher emphasises that yoga is a practice; that there is no end goal of having the perfect yoga routine. My friend has been trying to do a particularly difficult balance for years. She sometimes gets it for a second or two, but then falls. Her teacher says, "We all fall in life, the important thing is to get up and try again." The important thing is to believe it's possible. As Henry Ford said, "Whether you think you can or you think you can't, you're right."

Many years ago, I read something that I've applied so often in life and it's always helped me. I read that even if deep down inside you are crippled with fear just act as though you are confident. Simply walk tall, speak up, stand up straight and keep your shoulders back. You'll eventually feel as confident as you are pretending to be. If you want to get good at something, become a good actor and it will start coming true. Literally, act it. We've heard it before – you've got to fake it to make it – but it really is true. I've tried it and it works.

You can't let losing trades change your game. The process of losing trades is all part of the bigger picture. When we're trading, we're not playing one game, we're in it for the season. If a football team packed it in after losing one game, they'd be out of the league in weeks. They'd get nowhere. Every time we lose a game, we have to say, "We'll win the next one."

Sure, we learn lessons from the game we lost, but we don't focus on the actual final score. It's just one of several scores of the season, and the season's not over until it's over. We have to set our sights on the next game and prepare for that one, believing we can win it. This is exactly how you have to treat your trading experience.

Your losing trade is just a small part of the sample size. It's par for the course. You don't change your strategy because you've had one losing trade.

A bad manager is one who makes radical changes to his team after one losing game, despite that side having won many in the past. If he's constantly losing games, he needs to restructure, but if it's one game in a winning streak, he shouldn't change a thing.

Similarly, a bad trader is one who makes radical changes to his trading strategy after losing one trade despite having won many trades using that strategy. If he's constantly losing trades, he needs to adjust his plan, but if it's one loss in a winning streak, he shouldn't change a thing.

Even when you're 3-0 down, you can't give up, and if you lose, you can't take that loss with you into the next game or it will adversely affect your overall performance for the rest of your season. The sooner you learn to take the downs with the ups, the sooner you'll get really good at trading.

Conquering emotion

Am I telling you to take emotion out of the equation? Well, to a certain extent, yes. At the same time, you're human, so you can't actually be that trained monkey; you can't flip a switch and turn off emotion. What you can do is retrain your response to something. When you get to the stage where your feeling about a losing trade is the same as your feeling about a winning trade, you are becoming a good trader. It won't come naturally. You have to trick your brain into doing this.

You will remember in Part One I mentioned my first game at Anfield, the one where I fell apart when I was marking Craig Johnston – I lost my bottle and froze up. There was no physical reason for this. My emotions just took me off in the wrong direction. I hadn't learnt to master myself. I didn't know how to retrain my brain or trick it into feeling something different.

All those voices of doom and fear that sprung up in my mind, and that grew louder and louder as we got closer to the game, took over. If only I could have rerouted my emotions, I would have pulled through. But I didn't have that experience; I didn't have the necessary mental strength, at that point in my life, to do it. I wish we'd had mental training back in those days! My brain listened to a distorted emotional response instead of logic.

Logic decreed that my team were good enough to be playing in the country's top division otherwise why were we there? Logic decreed that I was good enough to be playing for this team, that I'd helped get promoted the previous season, otherwise why was I there? Logic decreed that there was always a chance of beating the team at the top of the league table, because other teams had done it in the past; there was always that possibility. And logic decreed that I was well prepared because I'd done all my training and had warmed up in the usual way.

There was nothing logical or factual that said I should be more afraid or nervous than in any other game except for the fact that it was Anfield and it was Liverpool, the best team in the country at that moment in time. I let these two things diminish all the logic I knew to be true.

My brain embraced an irrational, illogical emotion of fear. All fear said was, "Who do you think you are walking out on to this historic pitch and attempting to play against the greatest side in English football? You're not good enough to be here."

No matter who you are or what you do, you've probably experienced something similar, some moment, or some event, when you were put off your game by a nagging voice of insecurity, of self-doubt, of fear. What can you do about it? You have to learn to reroute the emotion or to retrain the thought pattern.

When you lose a trade, the voice in your head might say, "You bad person, you just lost money, that was good money, you could have paid a bill with that money and you just lost it, that was very irresponsible, and it's typical, because you can't be trusted with money, because when you were nine, you..." etc. etc. Clearly you need to do that exercise of writing down past bad experiences on paper and ripping it up again!

You have to retrain that voice to say, "Hey, you lost this trade, but that's great because every losing trade brings you closer, statistically, to a winning trade, and every experience of losing helps you build the courage to stick to the plan."

In her seminal book, *Feel The Fear and Do it Anyway*, Susan Jeffers tells us, "The way you use words has a tremendous impact on the quality of your life." She suggests replacing our usual internal script with, for example, "I could" instead of "I should", or "this is an opportunity" instead of "this is a problem", and "next time..." instead of "if only...". Most importantly, she says, "Shift from being afraid of making a mistake to being afraid of not making a mistake. If you are not making any mistakes, you are not learning or growing." If you keep doing the same old things in life, nothing will change. You have to push yourself harder.

Every time I stepped over the white line on to a football pitch, there was a voice in the back of my head telling me to be afraid. I used to push it away. At that game at Anfield I wasn't able to, it got the better of me. But I never let it get that loud again and eventually it did shut up.

Every time I stepped out on to the pitch, I knew there was no turning back; I just had to trust that I had the skills to do the job I had been given. I couldn't control the opposing team, I could only do what I had trained myself to do – play football to the best of my ability. Therefore, win or lose, I'd done everything I could have done. It's no different in trading.

Every time I go to click the mouse that will put a trade on, there is a voice in the back of my head telling me to be afraid, telling me I'm getting it wrong, that I'm going to fail. It tries to stop me, but I don't listen to it. Once I'm in a trade, it's like being out on the pitch, there's no turning back. I have to play the game until it's over, trusting my skills, trusting that I can head the ball when I need to, trusting that my indicators have signalled the best time to get into the trade. I can't control the opposition; I can't control the markets.

So, win or lose, I've done my best. That's all mum and dad ever told me to do.

CHAPTER TWENTY-SIX:

ON THE BENCH

Frustration of waiting

THERE IS NOTHING more frustrating for a young footballer at the top of his game than having to sit on the bench waiting to be put on. No matter what's going on out there on the pitch, you want to be part of it. Okay, if your team loses, a part of you feels a small sense of relief that you weren't involved, on the grounds that, "The man who didn't do anything, didn't do anything wrong." If your team wins though it's tough to have to accept the fact that you weren't part of it.

We all know people in life who sit on the bench voluntarily. They sit around doing nothing, but complaining about everything. They complain on Facebook, on Twitter, in the office, at parties, in the pub, but they don't do anything to change their situation.

When you actually want to be doing something, when you would love to be out there playing, with your destiny in your own hands, it's maddening when you can't be. Of course, whether you like it or not, your manager has put you on the bench for a reason. Maybe you're not fully fit after coming back from injury (as was my case after my neck injury), maybe you haven't been playing well. Whatever it is, there's often little you can do about it, you usually have to accept it and wait it out.

Now I have a guilty confession to make, but I'd challenge any footballer to say they feel otherwise. Whenever I was sitting on the bench, I couldn't help but let a small part of me hope for my team to start losing.

I know it's a terrible admission, but when you desperately want to play, the best chance you've got of being put on is if your team starts losing. The manager's not going to be in any hurry to substitute players when the team's winning. Yes, you want the team to win the match in the end, but a small, selfish part of you can't help thinking, "If we go down a couple of goals, I've got a better chance of getting on."

Trust me, it doesn't matter if Chelsea are winning or losing the game, Fernando Torres isn't sitting on the bench thinking about the hundred grand a week he's raking in. All he cares about is getting out on to that pitch so he can do what he loves doing – play football and, most of all, score goals.

It is just as frustrating when you have to be on the bench when you're trading. By this, I mean when there are no trades to enter, or stop losses to move, or profits to bank. When everything is slow and nothing interesting is happening. You have to trust your manager – if he's not putting you on, you're not needed – just like you have to trust your signals and your trading plan – if they're not telling you to do anything, you don't need to do anything. You also have to trust the other players who are out there scoring goals for your team; just like you have to trust your existing trades are out there making money for you.

I know the big excitement of trading is in the moment of making money, like the big excitement of playing football is in the moment of scoring a great goal, but you have to be a great manager at the same time as being a great player. If nothing needs to be done by you at a given moment time, put yourself on the bench.

Luckily, I didn't sit on the bench too often during my football career. I mostly played under managers who'd chosen me to be at the club themselves so they wanted me out there at the start of every game. This started to change at Sheffield, even before the neck injury, and it was tough.

The main problem was the turnover of managers. Howard Kendall had brought me to Sheffield United, but he left after my first season with the club. When the next manager got appointed, I had to prove myself again. This happened several times. By the time Neil Warnock arrived, I'd gone through five different managers in three years.

Early on in his managerial position, Warnock bought Keith Curle, who had just had a great four-year run at Wolves, captaining the team to their FA Cup semi-final against Arsenal in 1998. Unfortunately Keith played in my position, so he was obviously always going to be Neil's first choice. I found myself on the bench far too often and I had to really fight to get a game, especially after I returned following my neck injury. Despite this, Keith and I actually became great mates.

Keith had experienced his own share of frustration early on in his career. He'd been selected for the England squad for the Euro '92 competition, which proved disastrous; we didn't even progress beyond the group stage. Of course it wasn't Keith's fault personally, but perhaps partly because he was a member of that losing squad he never played for England again.

If you've stuck to your trading plan and you've lost money on a trade, it's not your fault, don't throw yourself off the team, or your strategy out of the squad. It may be that you have to sit on the bench for a while, but get back into the game when you get the next signal. Don't let past experience kill your confidence.

Constant readiness

Sitting on the bench is frustrating, of course. What's even worse is having no idea whether you are going to be there from one week to the next. Different managers have different schedules for announcing their starting 11. Some will tell you in the middle of the week that you're dropped for the next game. Sometimes, even if you're not told, it's obvious because of the training sessions. Sometimes the team sheet goes up the day before the game.

Sometimes you don't get told until an hour or so before the match! So you can't drop out of training; you might be needed. You can't sit back and eat a Big Mac while the rest of the squad are training; that's one way of guaranteeing you won't be picked.

So, even if there are no trades to enter, you must check your signals each day, you must keep money in your trading account so that when you get a signal to enter a trade there's the cash there ready to do it with. You can't just slack off all the training and preparation, just because you're on the bench for a couple of weeks.

It can be exhausting being in a perpetual state of readiness without getting the green light to do anything. It actually takes more effort than if you're pretty sure you'll be playing every game, but you can't let being on the bench deflate your spirit. There are players who start to give up once they've been put on the bench a few times. This is a defeatist attitude and could well lead to you never getting off the bench and back into the team ever again. Similarly, if you give up in trading just because your indicators are taking too long to give you any signals, then you are never going to make any money.

Back when I started playing professional football, managers would always start games with their best 11 players out on the pitch, without question. Now, with so many different competitions going on, both at home and in Europe, more and more managers are favouring squad rotation, for example starting with a different line-up on a Wednesday UEFA Cup game against an Italian side than the one that started against Spurs in their Sunday league game.

The players obviously don't like it, it's frustrating for top players to sit on the bench, especially if they had a particularly good game the last time the team played, but it is a kind of insurance, a way of keeping a larger pool of players fit and ready to play their best. If one of your best players was to get injured, you can substitute him with someone who's recently had experience, rather than someone who hasn't played a full 90 minutes for two months, which used to happen in the old days. You're not putting all your eggs in one basket so to speak.

Rafael Benitez is a manager who believes strongly in squad rotation. When he first arrived at Liverpool, his players were unhappy with the strategy, but they soon accepted it in light of their successful run under the Spaniard.

Rotation works in trading, too. If you put all your money on one trade this dramatically increases your risk. By spreading your money around on various trades in different markets, you're minimising your risk.

Say, for example, you have £1000 in your pot when you start out; think of that money as your whole squad. Your squad is basically £1000 and each player is £30 (3% of your trading account), so you've got around 33 players in your squad. First of all, you can't play the whole squad at one time because if any of them got injured you'd have no one to replace them. If each £30 is a player, you only put about eight players (around 20% of your squad) on the pitch at any one time. If you start losing, you might have to take some of those players off and put some new ones on.

Your signals will tell you when to put your players/trades on and when to take them off. If your trade is *injured* you don't keep it on the pitch, you close your trade out and let your *player* recover and live to fight another day. Keep healthy players/trades on the pitch and you have a good chance of winning the match. If you play the same 11 over and over even when they get injured – i.e. you don't even take them off when they are losing money and your signals are telling you to close out of the trade – then the game's as good as over.

Coming off the bench

Being on the bench when you're a defender is even more frustrating than being a forward. If you're at 2-2, the manager might put on a centre forward to go for the win; he might put some fresh blood out on the pitch, someone who's likely to score a goal. Unless your team's conceding a lot of goals, or someone's injured, a central defender's chances of being put on are pretty slim. However, there was that one time...

The game was Sheffield United vs. Bolton Wanderers, when 'Big' Sam Allardyce was their manager. I was on the bench and the score was 0-0. A few minutes before the end of the game, the manager put me on. A couple of minutes later, we got a corner kick. With the whistle about to go, the whole team were up at the attacking end, hoping to score that winning goal in the final minute. And guess who got his head on to the ball at exactly the right time?

That's right, it was me. I could hardly believe it; it was like a dream. As soon as we restarted, the final whistle blew and it was confirmed, I'd scored the winning goal and we'd won the match. It was the most amazing feeling. I remember being so frustrated at sitting on the bench for the majority of the game but my patience paid off in spades. As we were cooling down on the pitch after the game, I remember Sam came out and gave me a withering look. "You git, Sandford!" he said. "You git!" I couldn't stop smiling. It was the best feeling in the world.

So it can happen, that miraculous last-minute goal from someone (even a central defender) that comes seemingly out of the blue. Follow your signals, be patient, stick to your guns and you never know, you might be surprised one day.

Patience is key

Patience will serve you so well in trading. You have to get good at waiting. If you know you're someone who struggles with patience, get some other hobby that you can do when you're waiting for signals to go off. Keep those itchy fingers away from the keyboard.

There's a kind of fictional image that people have of the trading room floor being this crazy, frantic place. In real life, things usually happen at a much slower pace, requiring the patience of a saint.

Do you remember the scene of the frantic trading room floor in *Trading Places*? It's one of my favourite films. Right near the end (spoiler alert!), the Dukes believe they are going to corner the Orange Juice Market because they think they've seen the crop report ahead of time saying yields will be low. But Valenine (Eddie Murphy) and Winthorpe (Dan Aykroyd) have switched the report.

On the trading room floor, the Dukes start buying OJ futures; other traders follow, driving up the price. All the while, Valentine and Winthorpe are selling futures at this inflated price because they know that the crop report shows yields will be normal. Indeed, when the report is announced, the price nosedives. Valentine and Winthorpe then make a killing buying back futures at the lower price from everyone except the Dukes. The Dukes have obviously bought on leverage and fail to meet a margin call of several millions, which bankrupts them.

It's actually a great scene to watch if you're struggling to understand short selling and margin calls. You'll see it all happen when you watch the film.

In real life, there is rarely that mad feeding frenzy in the markets. You have time to set up your trades and you have so much time when you have to wait for things to happen. Even day traders often have to be extremely patient and do nothing while they wait for their selected indicators to trigger a move to buy or sell. The hardest part can be when there seems to be a fast moving market but you're not getting a signal to do anything. That's like being on the bench in a high-scoring game. You desperately want to be out there, soaking up some of the fast-paced action, but your time hasn't come yet. Frustrating, to say the least.

I have a friend who works on the technical side of the film business. He tells me there's this phrase they use on set, which is, "Hurry up and wait." It means that everyone has to be ready, everything in place, for the director to get the shot. The shot might not happen for half a day but you still have to be ready, for hours, for the director to call, "Action!"

CHAPTER TWENTY-SEVEN:
THE OFFSIDE RULE

The rule

IN FOOTBALL, A player is in an offside position if any part of his body that can legally touch the football is past the second-last defender (the last usually being the goalkeeper) in the opposition's half of the pitch, at the time that the ball is played to him by a teammate who is behind him on the pitch. He is not committing an offside offence if he:

1. is not interfering with play,

2. is not interfering with an opponent,

3. does not use his offside position as an advantage in any way (for example touching a ball that rebounds off the goal, the keeper or any other opponent), and

4. is receiving the ball from a throw-in, corner or goal kick.

It's not just the deciding on the split-second moment a player becomes offside, it's the arbitrary nature of all of the above that causes endless disputes. As well as judging whether the player is in an offside position, the referee has to decide if an offence has been made.

Of course, the most likely scenario is that he is interfering with play in some way otherwise he wouldn't be so close to the goal, but the debate rages on. Alan Hansen is forever complaining on TV that in given situations a player should not have been ruled offside because he wasn't interfering in play.

So, now you understand what it means to be offside, you will be able to understand how to use the offside rule in a tactical way. (Don't worry, we'll establish the relevance to trading soon, but in the meantime you'll be able to show off in the pub with your expert knowledge of the offside rule!)

Choosing tactics for the situation

Obviously, in football, you change your tactics according to the team you're up against. You figure out where the opposition's strength comes from and you play against them accordingly. For example, with some forwards, you get your defenders as high up the pitch and as far away from the goal as possible so that the forwards can't get too close to the goal without risking getting into an offside position.

Of course this tactic won't work with a really fast player because, even from an onside position, if they get the ball they will likely run past you. But it works well against a player like Peter Crouch.

Crouch isn't that fast, but he's lethal up near the goal because he's a giant, towering over most defenders at 6'7". All his teammates need to do is get the ball in the air and Crouch is going to head it in. You're in particular danger if you give away a corner. When you're trying to defend a corner kick with Peter Crouch on the opposing side, the odds are stacked against you! So you want to keep your defenders high up the pitch so that Crouch has to stay far away from the goal, so that you've got more time to tackle him if he gets the ball and tries to run with it.

With a faster player, say someone like Tottenham's Aaron Lennon, this tactic just won't work. Lennon, who has played for Spurs since 2005 and has 20 England caps, is considered one of the fastest wingers in the Premier League today. It's dangerous to try and keep him up the pitch because you are only creating space for him to run into and he's likely to outrun any defenders in his path. You want to keep your defenders closer to goal so he can't get in behind them. You also need to defend against the players he could be passing to, as he's an expert at setting up goal-scoring opportunities for other strikers.

And then there's Giggsy Gonzales, with the fastest run in the North West. I remember the first time I played against Ryan Giggs. I'd been feeling very apprehensive in the run up to the game; I had this vision of coming face to face with him when he had the ball and him leaving me for dust. Sure enough, when the moment came, that's exactly what happened.

It was like a slow-motion film clip: Giggs approaching me, me running towards him, then him dodging past me before I could even exhale, and running on towards goal, where he probably scored. It literally felt as if he left me spinning on the spot, letting out a slowed down, long, deep cry of "Noooooo!" It was like an out-of-body experience; I just felt this wind go past me as if it was the air displaced by a bullet. I was the coyote and Giggs was the roadrunner.

You see, there's something to be said about the power of visualisation. I was so sure I could picture the exact scenario that was going to happen and when the moment came, every detail happened exactly as I had imagined it. Perhaps I should have visualised doing the perfect tackle and getting the ball off him.

The main point here is to show how footballers use different strategies in defence against different players. It's exactly the same in trading; you use different strategies to play different markets.

Strategy in the markets

Anyone can make money in a bullish market. If the market is going up, there is money to be made. It's harder to make money in a choppy market (one that's moving sideways, with no clear direction). However, the easiest market to make money in, as long as you use the right tactics, is one that is trending down; because this is when there is most movement and, remember, that's what we want. Bearish markets move faster because investors are panicking and trying to liquidate their positions quickly, thinking that they are losing too much too quickly.

So again, we're talking about timing. Imagine the markets are your opponents. You're a striker trying to get a goal and the markets are luring you into a trade too early, or at the wrong point. It's like the markets are trying to play you offside.

Markets don't often trend; they mostly move sideways or within a range, and you never know what they're going to do on a given day. In addition, individual markets behave differently. The gold market behaves very differently from other commodities and the forex market behaves completely differently from the stock market. That's why you need your trading indicators.

At least in football you know the team you are going to be playing in advance, so you more or less know which players you will be playing against. These days, managers send their scouts out well in advance to watch closely how teams are playing: who's looking strong up front, where the weakness in their defence might be, etc. It's vital to know as much about the opposing team as possible.

When I was at Portsmouth and we got into the top division, I remember having a recurring nightmare that we'd trained hard all week to face Manchester United, picking our tactics according to the players we knew we'd be facing, then on the Saturday we'd turn up and Liverpool would walk out on to the pitch. Impossible in football, but that's exactly how the markets behave.

You can do everything in your power to predict what's going to happen, you can send out your scouts (your charts) to gather up as much information as possible on how the markets are *playing*, but at any moment a whole different team could show up on the pitch, and you have to do as best you can with the risk management strategy you've put into place.

You have to tailor your strategy according to what's happening in front of you. In a trending market, you can go for bigger moves, and make more profits. In a choppy market, a range-bound market, you have to adjust your tactics accordingly.

If you play your tactics for a trending market in a range-bound market, you're going to lose. It's like playing against Giggs with your Crouch-based tactics. If you play Giggs offside and try to keep him up the field, you're just helping him win because you're leaving space for him to run into. One size doesn't fit all, in football or in trading.

You need as much information as possible about who you are playing against at any given moment. Once you've got your information on your charts, you must let your strategy dictate how you play. Play according to what your signals tell you to do; they are your scouts. Don't go off and play however you want to play, disregarding what the signals tell you to do, or you are likely to lose.

Trust your information. Stick to your tactics. Play the way you're instructed to play. That's the best way to reach the highest score.

CHAPTER TWENTY-EIGHT:
THE LONG GAME VS. THE SHORT GAME

STICKING WITH FOOTBALL tactics, let's break the game down to the smallest level: the pass. When you play a game made up of short passes, the short game, you have accuracy on your side. You are more likely to keep the ball, less likely to be tackled, and, by keeping possession, you are more assured of controlling the game (although if you pass the ball too much without moving it down the pitch, you start to increase the odds of the opposition intercepting and taking the ball away from you). It might take a little longer to get the ball down to the goal, but you're playing it safe, you're completing most of your passes.

When you play the short game in trading, by taking several small profits on small movements, you allow your profits to add up very slowly and you protect yourself from any big losses. The shorter the time you stay in the trade, the less likely you are to make any big profit, but the less likely you are to lose your money. (Not always, but in general.)

The long game is faster but more risky. In football you are trying to get the ball down the field as fast as possible. You risk being intercepted, you risk the ball going out of play, but the chances are worth taking because you are taking the ball right up to the goal quickly and if you have a forward in the right position, he might just knock it in for a goal.

In trading, if you stay in a trade for a long time, you are leaving more time for the price to keep rising and therefore make you a greater profit over a longer time period. You also risk the possibility of the price dropping and then continuing to fall over a long period, possibly to the point where you are out of the trade because you hit your stop loss. The longer you leave your trade on, the greater chance you've got of hitting a higher target, but the more you risk something going wrong.

In football, we're looking at each pass; in trading we're looking at each decision. Based on what's best for you and your team, you need to choose whether to play a long game or a short game. Only you know which game you would be more comfortable playing, which game best suits your skills and temperament.

The shorter the game you play, the closer you come to operating as a *day trader*, which requires a greater investment of time. Do you have that time? You also have to be strong enough to take the emotional rollercoaster of ups and downs hour by hour. Do you have the thick skin necessary to bounce back quickly from losses and keep playing?

The longer the game you play, the more you start behaving like a *long-term investor*, where you keep your money in trades for long periods of time. Do you have the patience for this? You also risk losing your future nest egg if the markets were to collapse. If you put all your money into one stock, or one currency pair, you are exposing your future to the fluctuations of the market without much control. Are you happy with that kind of risk?

And this is why I recommend starting out in the middle ground, as a *swing trader*, so we're playing with a mix of some safe short passes and some riskier long balls. This works at the management level too.

Take two of the most successful teams in the Premier League today, Arsenal and Chelsea. We are accustomed to seeing both teams in the top half of the Premier League table, but they have almost opposite management strategies.

Arsenal has a history of keeping its managers for a very long time. Arsène Wenger has been with the club for 17 years and his management of the squad also takes the long-term approach, favouring the development of young players through the youth system rather than buying expensive players from other clubs; his philosophy being one of building a rock solid foundation so that the squad becomes a tight unit over time. Wenger plays the long game in his management strategy and it works.

Chelsea, on the other hand, seems to change managers as often as its kit, with most of them struggling to stay more than a season or two. Indeed, since Roman Abramovich took ownership of the club in 2003, there have been ten managers in as many years. There is also a huge turnover of players, with the focus on buying the best, and thus most expensive, players in the world to create a team with the best skills possible. In his first term at the club, José Mourinho virtually had carte blanche and an open chequebook to buy any player he wanted and under his (relatively long) three-year management, Chelsea won the Premier League title twice, the FA Cup and two League Cups. The club wants quick results and will do whatever it takes to get them. Abramovich plays the short game with Chelsea and it works.

Both strategies work, but each is suited to a different personality. As clubs, Chelsea and Arsenal definitely have very different personalities. Who are you? What's your personality? Do you get stressed easily? Are you motivated by short-term gains for a long-term goal or are you better at building slowly and waiting for your moment in the sun? You need to know who you are, you need to know your strengths and weaknesses before you choose your strategy.

Remember, the shorter or the faster the game, the more magnified your responses become. If you are emotionally affected by losing money, if you can't cut off your emotions and see loss as part of the process, then you are probably not suited to playing a very short game and you need to do extra mental preparation for dealing with the rollercoaster of trading. Are you a confident risk taker? If not then, again, you need to do some mental preparation to convince yourself that some risk is necessary if you are going to try to make money trading the markets.

Having said all that, the most likely scenario if you've never traded before is that you don't know what kind of a personality you have when it comes to money, or you can't be honest with yourself about it. Perhaps deep down you disrespect money; perhaps on some level you are scared of having too much of it because you don't trust yourself to spend it wisely; perhaps you have some deep-rooted subconscious relationship with it you don't even know about.

While you are finding out how you respond to trading, while you are learning about your relationship with money, it's best to keep things simple but quite fluid, so you can learn the lessons and find out what works best for you.

That's why I recommend beginners start by:

- *Swing trading*, to give them enough activity on a daily basis but not so much that it becomes overwhelming and takes over their life,
- *Spread betting* to keep things simple, make tax-free profits and produce faster results with less initial outlay; and trading the
- *Forex markets* because unlike stocks and shares, currencies are highly unlikely to suddenly plummet to zero (as we have seen some companies do).

CHAPTER TWENTY-NINE:
HOOLIGANS AND #$%@* #ANKERS

WHETHER OR NOT you personally enjoy it, football – the beautiful game – is a huge part of England's national heritage and we should be proud of all our achievements in the sport, in the domestic leagues, in European club competitions and at an international level.

However, there was a depressing time in England when football was synonymous with hooliganism. Organised groups of troublemakers spoilt it for everyone else by using the game as a vehicle for thuggery and vandalism. There was a real crackdown against criminal behaviour in the late 1980s and 1990s, and these days English fans usually outshine their European counterparts in terms of behaviour at big international matches.

In a similar (albeit less physical) way, some bankers gave investing a bad name when it emerged that some exceptionally clever corruption and a total abuse of financial deregulation had led to the banking crisis of 2007-2008. Since that time, we have seen some of these bad practices, such as the big PPI scandal and mis-sold interest-rate swaps, exposed in the media, with the public being offered fair compensation for the money they were cheated out of.

To begin with, when the property bubble burst and the banks started going under, the public assumed we had hit a recession similar to that of the 1930s, the one that led up to the Second World War. It was scary, but it was an economic pattern. Or so they thought.

Now we know the truth – that people were cheated out of millions by corrupt institutions. The average man on the street can no longer be sure who to trust. It's depressing, but if it makes people more proactive and hands-on when it comes to their investments and savings, maybe it's not such a bad thing.

Those of us who were part of the football community were not prepared to stand by and let the hooligans give it a bad name. Similarly economic growth, from a personal to a global scale, is important. We must not let corrupt bankers give it a bad name.

Of course, football continues to hit the headlines. There will always be a few young lads who get misled and corrupted by the money and fame, but they are a tiny minority. In all my years of playing professional football, while I might have seen some over-exuberant celebrating on the odd occasion, I never met anyone or saw anything I was shocked or disgusted by. You don't hear much about the normal, hard-working footballers from good families in happy marriages because their stories don't sell newspapers like the antics of the odd juvenile bad boy.

Contrary to what the tabloids would have you believe, being a young footballer player does not make you a drug-taking, adulterous thug. Likewise, being a trader does not make you one of the greedy, ruthless, conniving opportunist bankers who brought down the financial industry. Yes, there will always be people who abuse their positions, there will always be troublemakers, but none of them should stop you enjoying football or making money.

It's your life and you can do anything with it, as long as it's legal, and as long as you do it with integrity. As with any system, where there is a winner, there is also a loser. But when you win in trading, the only people who lose are the spread betting companies, and they wouldn't be in business if they weren't winning huge sums of money in the long term.

Spread betting companies make money because 80% of people lose. Why? Not because it's risky, of course it's risky, but because they don't make the right choices. If you make the right choices you will be part of the 20% who make money trading.

Using good charts and trading indicators in spread betting is like being allowed to use a computerised card counter in poker. If you did this in poker you'd win too often, which is why it wouldn't be allowed. In spread betting you are allowed the machine that calculates the probability of you winning but most people don't know how to use it. If you could learn how, why wouldn't you?

I've said before that we stand to make most money when markets are bearish (falling). They fall because investors have pumped them up. They fall fast because of the panic that spreads among investors who are scrambling to get out of their long positions. It's like climbing up the stairs and falling out of a window – you climb steadily and fall fast. It took six years for the markets to build up to the level they got to in 2008. It took six weeks for them to crash. Greed makes markets rise gradually. Fear makes them fall fast.

Talking vs. delivering

Many people get into the world of finance because they want to talk the talk; very few actually learn to walk the walk. I call it the "dinner party syndrome". You go to a dinner party and you overhear people talking about the markets. They love to quote this newspaper or that newspaper, and half the time I listen to them knowing that the markets are actually doing the exact opposite of what they are talking about.

It's the same with Bloomberg and CNBC and all those financial news programmes. I often see some big shot company director being interviewed, talking about how well his company is doing, when in reality the share price is crashing and the only reason he's on the show talking up the company is because he's in trouble. I view it all as light entertainment!

The only way you can see what is really happening is by looking at the real-time charts in your chart package, showing the actual movements of the markets. Everything else is background noise, and some of it can be dangerously misleading.

It's easy to talk a great game, but you have to deliver. When Kevin Keegan was managing Newcastle United in the mid-1990s, he famously got goaded into an outburst during a live TV interview about Sir Alex Ferguson, saying, "I would love it if we beat them. Love it!" Newcastle and Man United were neck and neck in the race for the Premiership title. Keegan talked a great game, but it was all hot air. Newcastle failed to deliver and Man United went on to win the title.

Kenny Dalglish succeeded Keegan and was the manager during that FA Cup semi-final game between Sheffield United against Newcastle at Old Trafford that I've mentioned a couple of times. After the game, I took a friend's young football-mad son down to the pitch to have a walk around. We bumped into Kenny Dalglish as he was heading back to Newcastle's changing room and I asked him if he'd sign this young lad's programme. He said he would with pleasure.

We thanked him and were about to leave when he said, "You two, follow me." He took us back to the changing room and Shearer was still sitting in there. This kid was speechless. Kenny picked up Shearer's shirt and threw it over to the kid. "Here," he said, "you can keep that." That moment really struck a chord with me. Kenny didn't need to do any of that. He was just being a really decent guy and making a young boy's dream come true.

At the end of the day, it doesn't matter how much money you have, it matters how you live your life. The only person who can be a good judge of whether you're doing that right is you. Your integrity should be your only yardstick for success.

FINAL WORD

As I said in the introduction, I decided to write this book for a number of reasons.

Predominantly, I felt that I had something useful to say. I hope you agree! I believe my ideas and experience can help people to get ahead faster than if they stumble over the stepping-stones of experience alone. If I can reduce the time in which it takes people to learn how to make a decent monthly income from trading, that can only be a good thing.

On a personal level, I also wanted a new challenge. I can play football; I can trade the money markets. I wanted to see if a person from Elephant and Castle who left school at 16 with no academic qualifications could write a book.

Years ago, when I was a footballer, when I was just beginning to dabble in a few investments, I felt intimidated by people who I perceived to be smarter and more successful than me. I thought you needed big qualifications, an MBA, a degree in accountancy or economics, to be a successful trader. I soon found out that's not true.

The more I got to know people in the financial world, the more I realised they were all full of the same insecurities and fears as the next person. I didn't need to feel inferior to them anymore. I realised that trading was a true meritocracy.

Recently, the public has had its eyes opened to what really goes on in the banking world. The LIBOR scandal and the exposure of invalid PPI schemes have shown that not all bankers are honest. People are getting angry. I remember getting angry when I realised that the *big guys* were cheating the *little guys* out of money. Since having my eyes opened to what's really been going on, I've had this strong desire to see the little guy fight back.

There's a common perception that wealth is about having material things, but I see wealth simply as a key to freedom. The more money I have, the more stability I have, and the more time I have to devote to my family, to spend with my children. Isn't that worth working hard for?

More wealth buys you more time, and time is precious. We never know how much of it we have. I'd give anything to turn back the clock and spend more time with my mum; I had no idea how little I was going to have.

Why do so many of us waste time on things we don't enjoy doing? If you get up every morning and go to a job you love, then fine; but if you don't, then it's up to you to change things. It's so easy to get into the rat race and get trapped and become too afraid to leave. We drag ourselves out of bed, commute and spend long hours behind a desk doing something we don't enjoy.

We have come to live in a society where we don't have time for each other anymore. What's the point in living like that? If we're not having a good, healthy relationship with our family members and friends then something's gone wrong. That's not living, that's just existing. What's stopping us from taking more control, from going out to find a way of making more money in less time, to buy us more time to have a better quality of life?

My years of teaching people to trade the markets have shown me that the number one reason why people struggle financially is because they have a distorted relationship with money. Nine times out of ten, they are not even aware that this is going on, but if you dig deep enough, you will find some experience in their past that has affected the way they think about money.

This often leaves them with a subconscious fear of having a lot of money, like they don't trust themselves to be wealthy. Sometimes I get the feeling that they perceive wealthy people to be categorically dishonest and ruthless, and they don't want to become one of those people. Or it could be that they were brought up to believe that it is not possible for people like them to acquire considerable wealth without winning the lottery.

I strongly believe that the first battle people need to win, before they can begin to think about increasing their wealth, is to dispel all their preconceived attitudes towards money, to cut the ties that bind them to their past experiences and patterns – to give themselves a clean slate, a fresh start and a positive attitude.

What most of us fail to acknowledge is that we are all basically the same. Look at any successful person out there – look at Richard Branson, or Peter Jones from *Dragons' Den*, or Gary Lineker – and I assure you that they, too, have had their moments of fear and insecurity, those moments when that little voice whispers in their head, "You can't do this." The only difference between them and those who are not as successful as they want to be is that they've taught themselves to ignore that voice. They hear that voice of doubt and they forge on regardless.

Many people see their commitments as some kind of sentence that's been imposed upon them, they refuse to see that, in a free society, they always have choices, they may just have to get out of their comfort zone to see them. Everyone gets nervous at times, everyone experiences moments of self-doubt, everyone is afraid of failure, but there is no better feeling than proving those voices of doom wrong when you achieve your goals.

Every day I meet people who just let life happen to them. They've got themselves into a comfortable, safe pattern and they stick to it even if it makes them miserable. They never stop complaining about the things they haven't got, but they don't do anything to change their situation because they are afraid.

It's not what happens to you in life, it's how you deal with it that counts. It's only your attitude that will shape your future.

* * *

I hope that at the very least this book has inspired you. If it has, then I've achieved what I set out to do. Even if trading the money markets is not for you, or it's not the right time for you to dive in, I hope you believe that there is a real, viable, way of making money out there that you can be in control of, and that you don't need any fancy qualifications to be good at it.

It doesn't matter whether or not you actually end up trading, what matters is that you know you could if you wanted to. I hope I've got my main message across, which is that anyone can do it.

If you are ready to start trading and you need more guidance, I'm here, ready, willing and able to be your mentor. You'll find more information about the courses that I run and the services I provide on the Trading College website:

www.tradingcollege.co.uk

I know, personally, how important it is to have good mentors and role models. I've been lucky enough to have some great mentors who've helped me shape my life, starting with my very first mentor, my old footballing dad, the late Alan Ball. He inspired me and set me on a path of honest, disciplined hard work towards becoming the best footballer I could be. Since then, I've met many people who've inspired me, both in football and in trading. Now I'd like to pay it forward.

I've already achieved some great goals in my life.

My new goal is to help others achieve theirs.

INDEX

COMPLETE YOUR HARRIMAN HOUSE TRADING LIBRARY

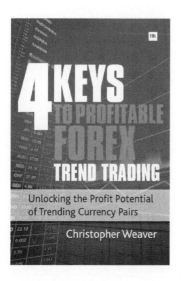

4 Keys to Profitable Forex Trend Trading

Unlocking the Profit Potential of Trending Currency Pairs

By Christopher Weaver

"An excellent resource for forex traders and investors."

FX Trader Magazine

Available as paperback and eBook

---

101 Ways to Pick Stock Market Winners

By Clem Chambers

"101 pithy and personally researched tips which help day traders, investors and stock pickers of every kind to focus in on what characterises a potentially successful stock."

Available as paperback

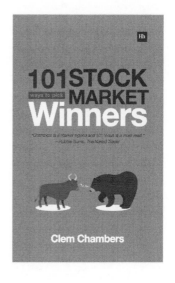

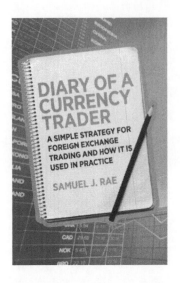

Diary of a Currency Trader

A simple strategy for foreign exchange trading and how it is used in practice

By Samuel J. Rae

"A no-nonsense, full disclosure look at trading the forex markets."

Available as paperback and eBook

Kathleen Brooks on Forex

A simple approach to trading foreign exchange using fundamental and technical analysis

By Kathleen Brooks

"A great foundation for new traders; a succinct review for those who have been trading for some time."

Available as paperback and eBook

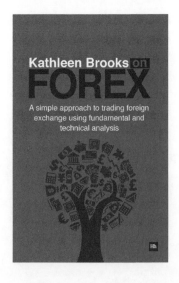